# There Are No Words

## The Walls are Talking

# Street Art of Valparaíso

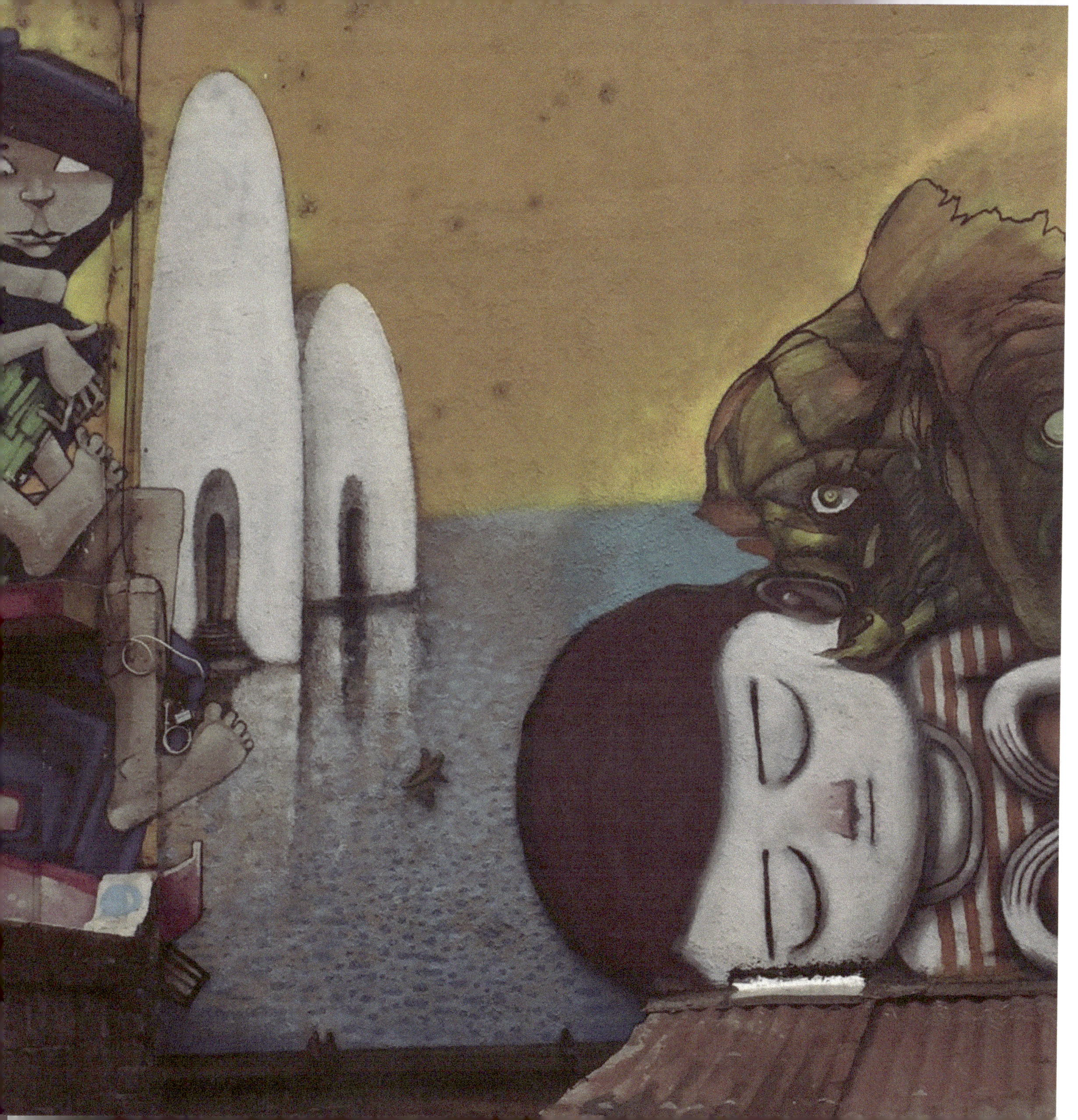

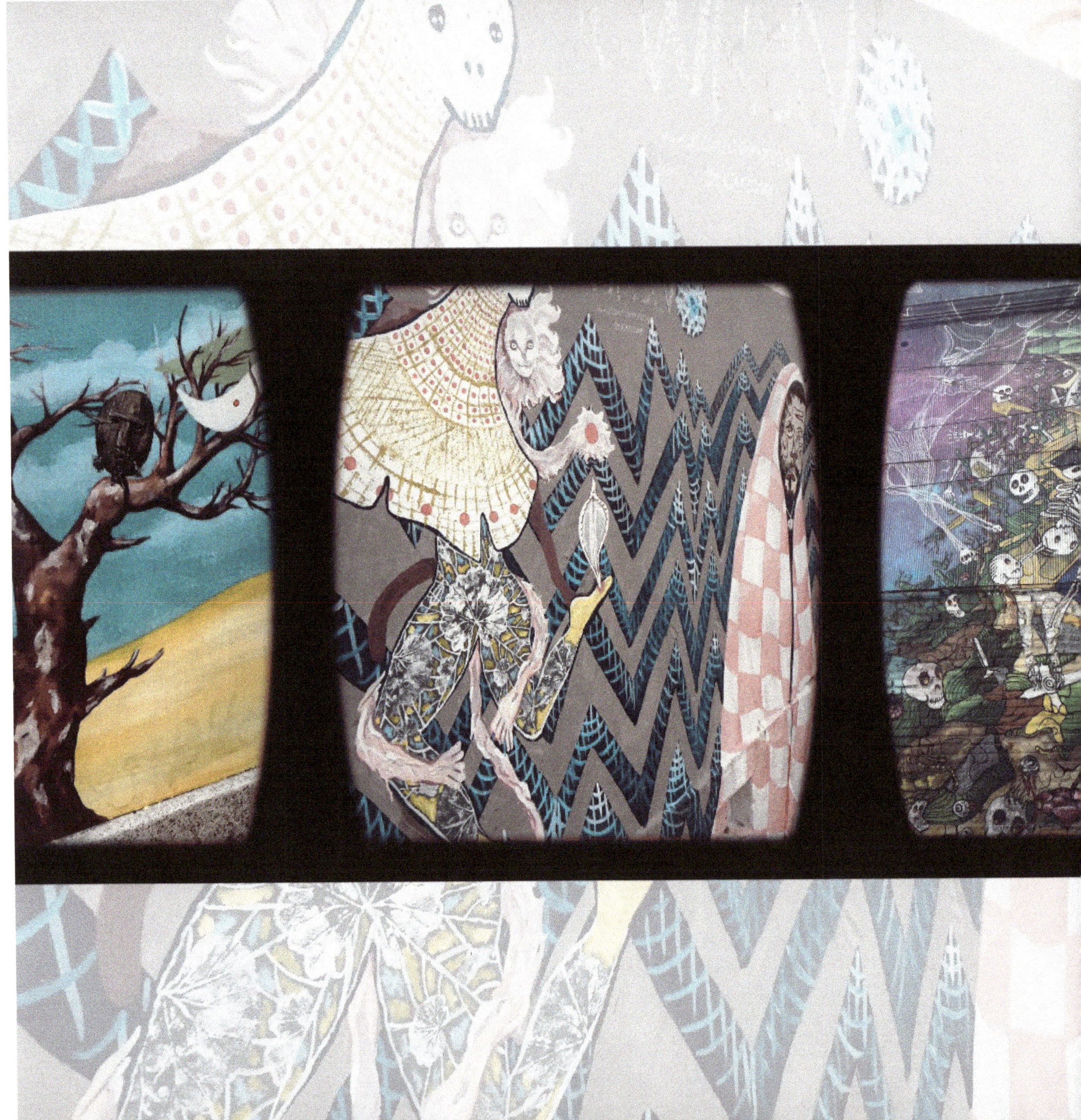

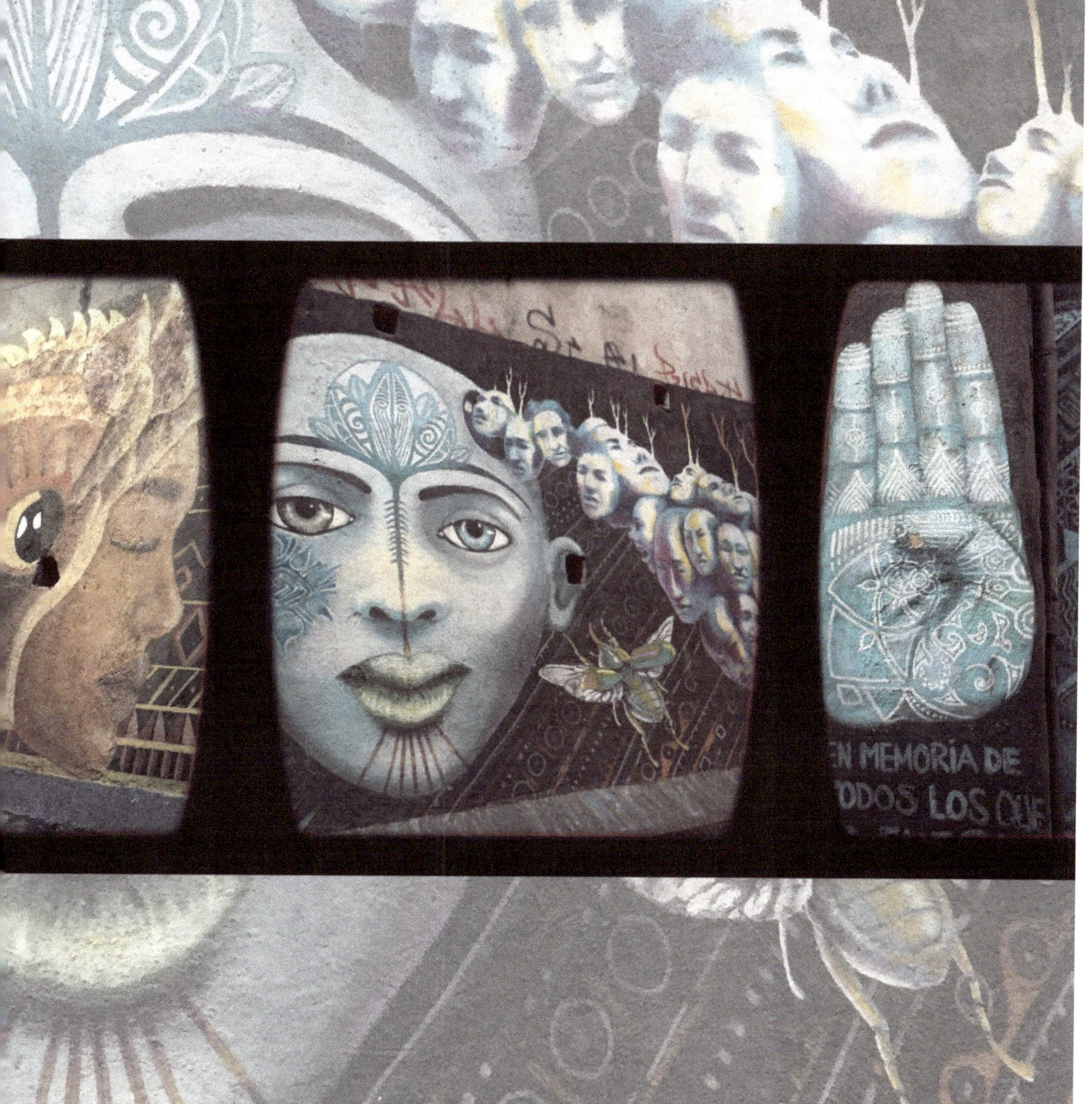

EN MEMORIA DE
TODOS LOS QUE

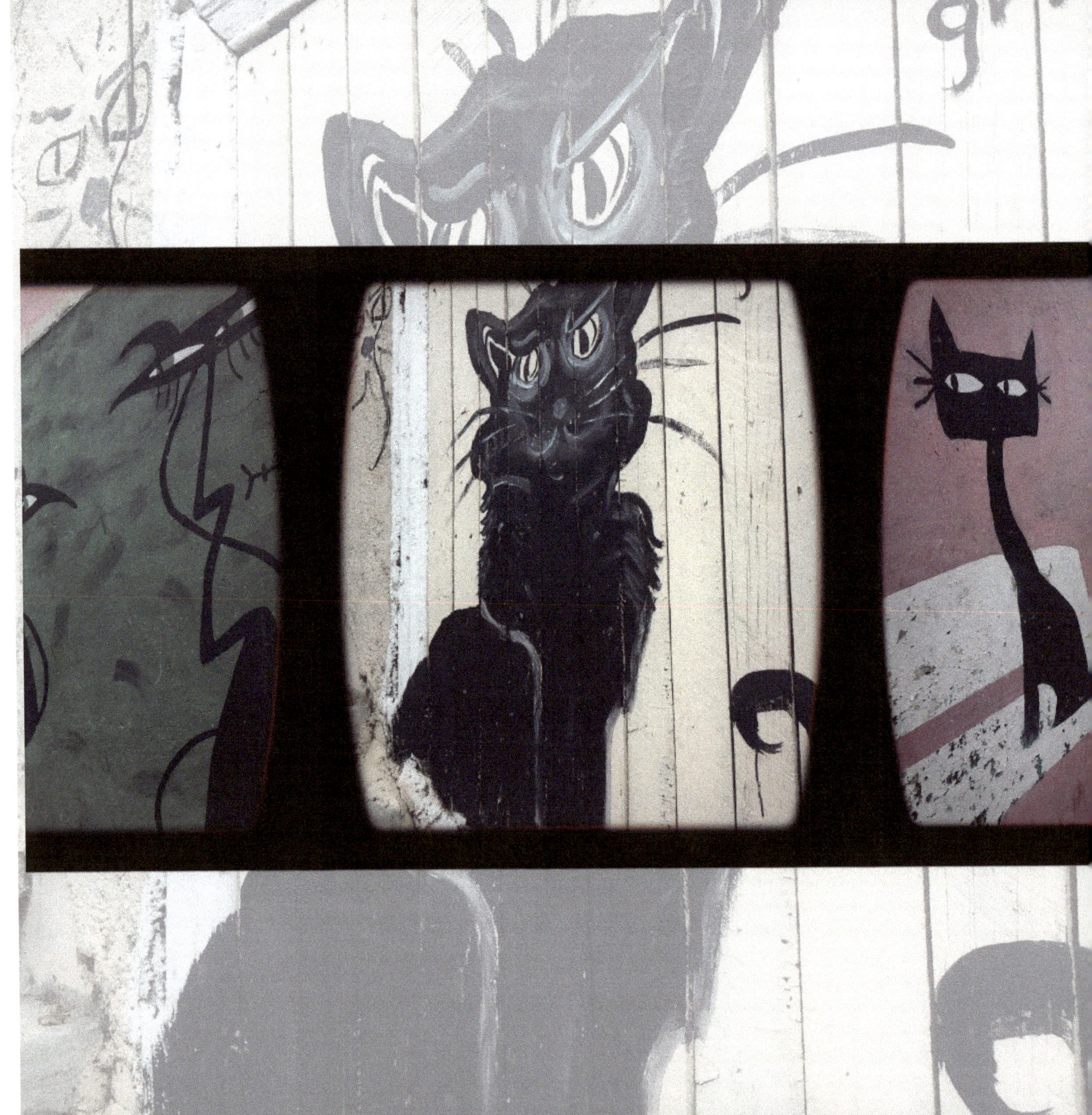

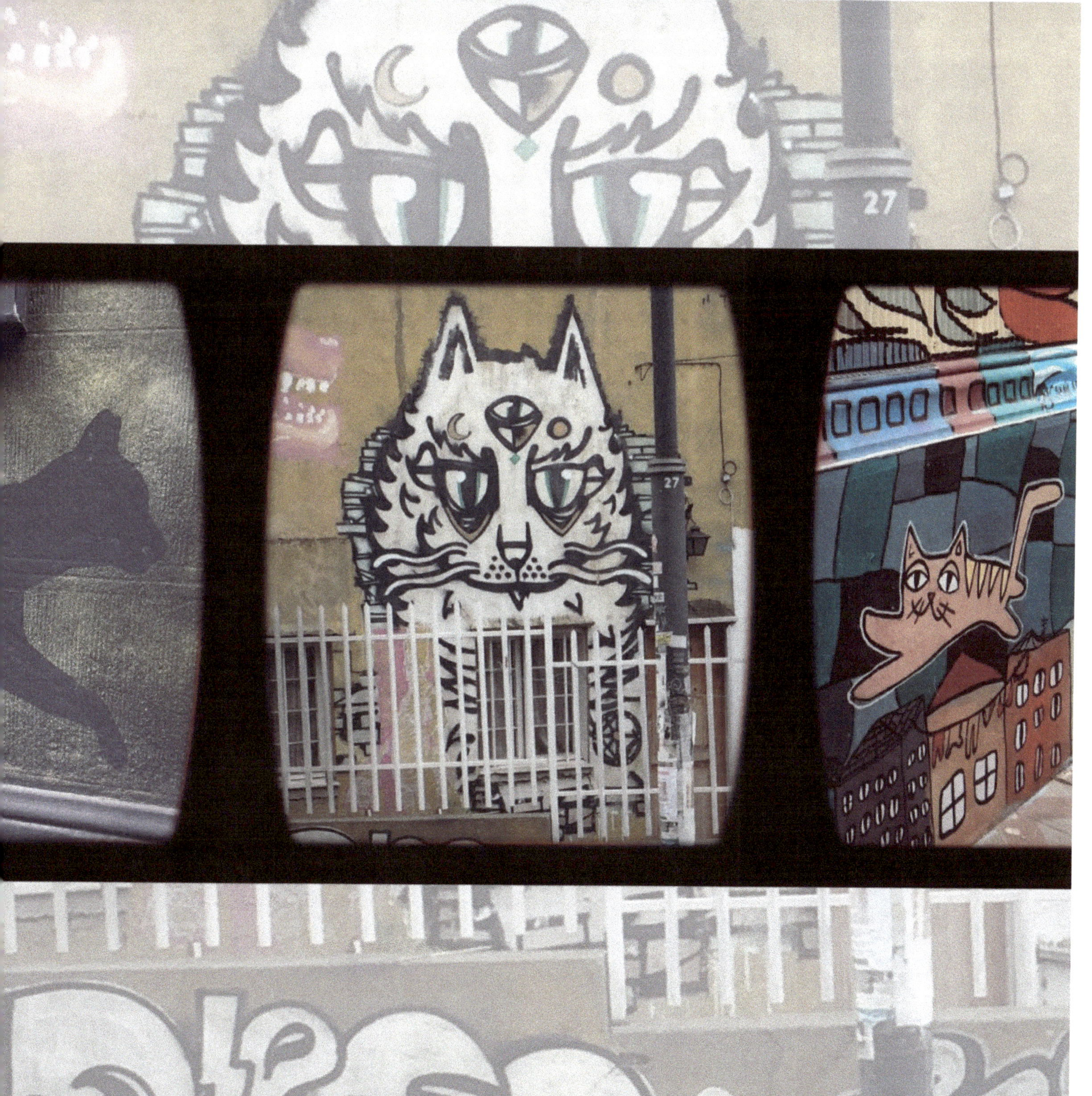

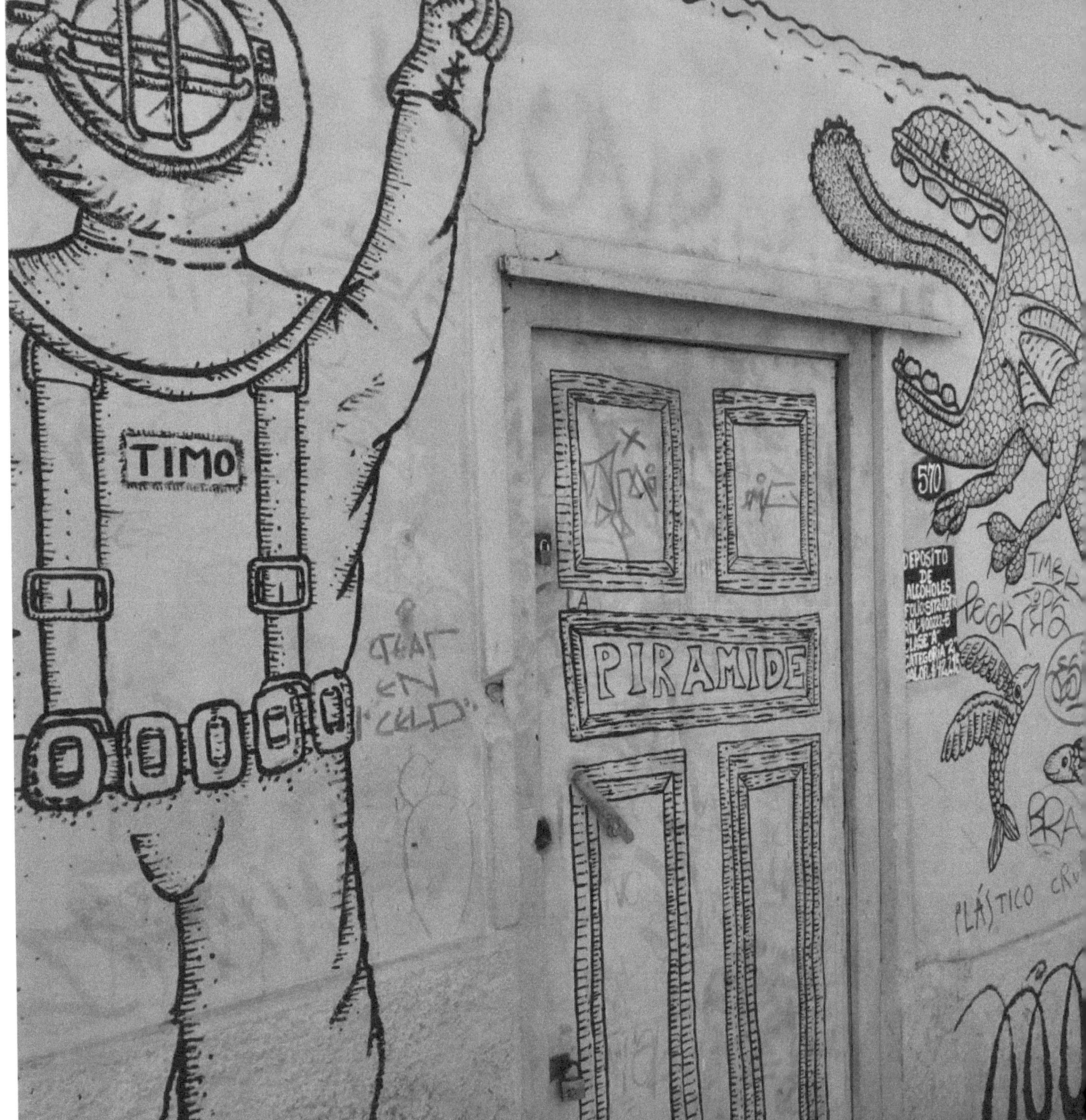

TIMO
PIRAMIDE
570
DEPOSITO
DE
ALCOHOLES
PLÁSTICO

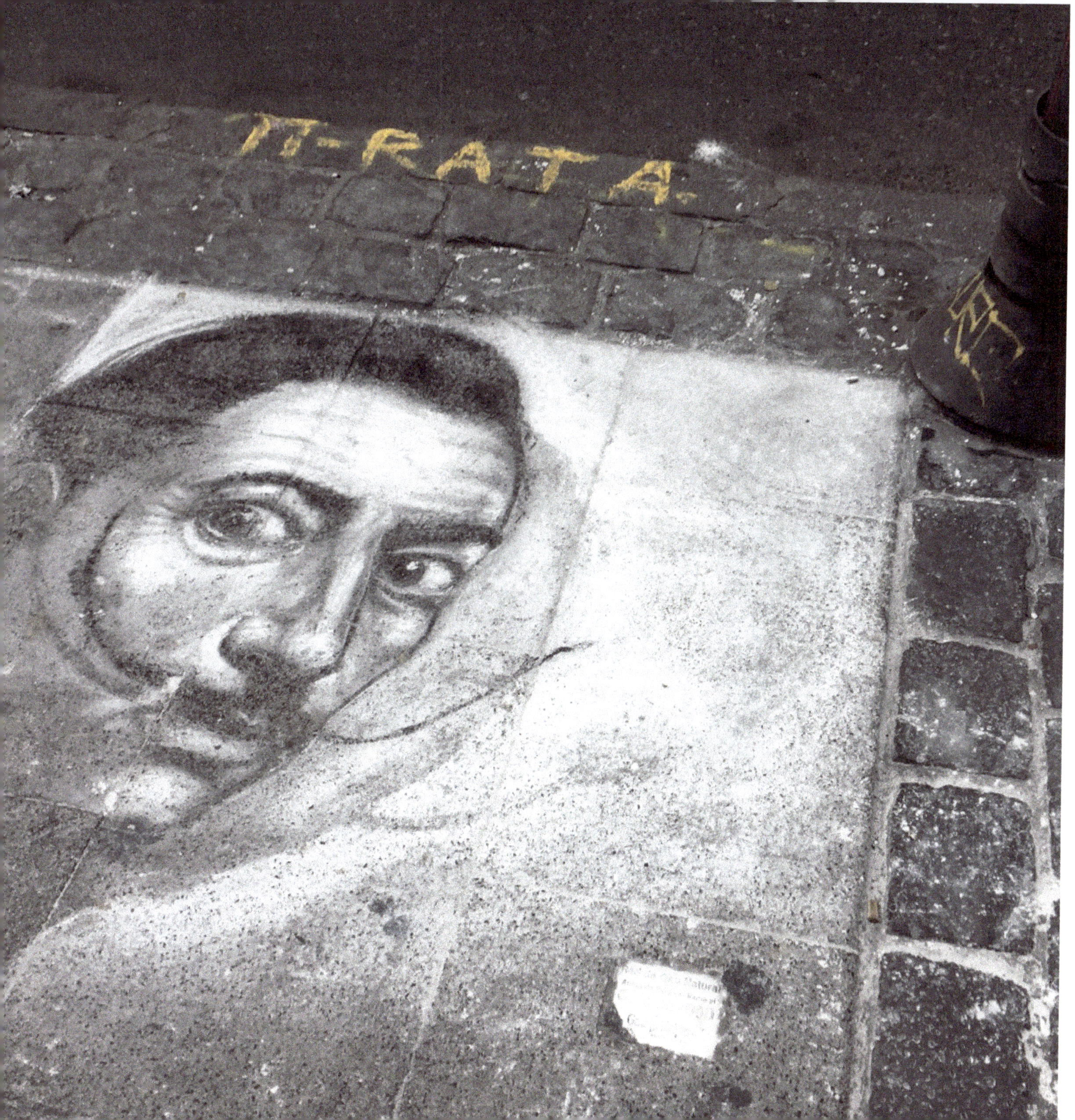
π-RATA.

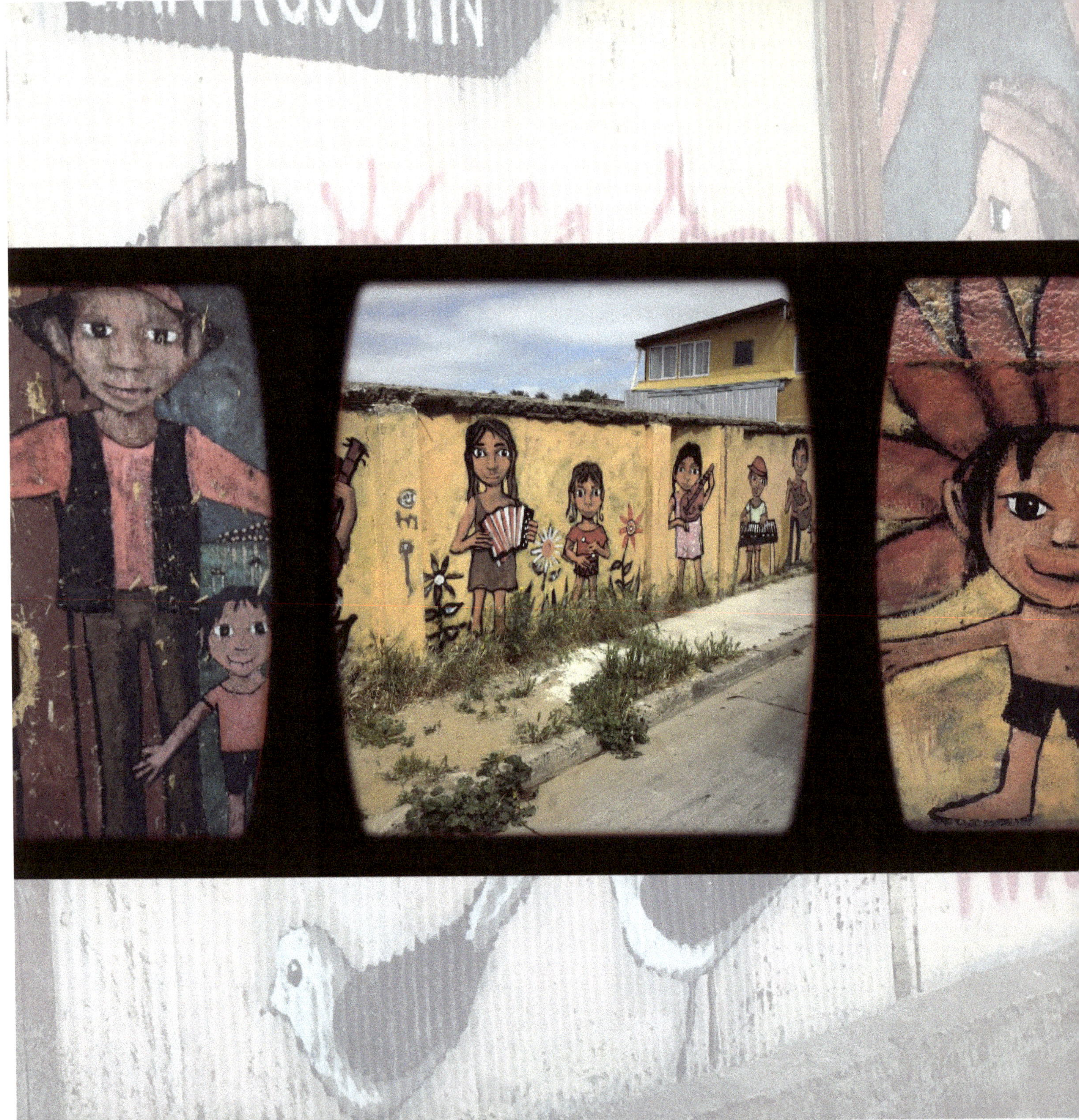

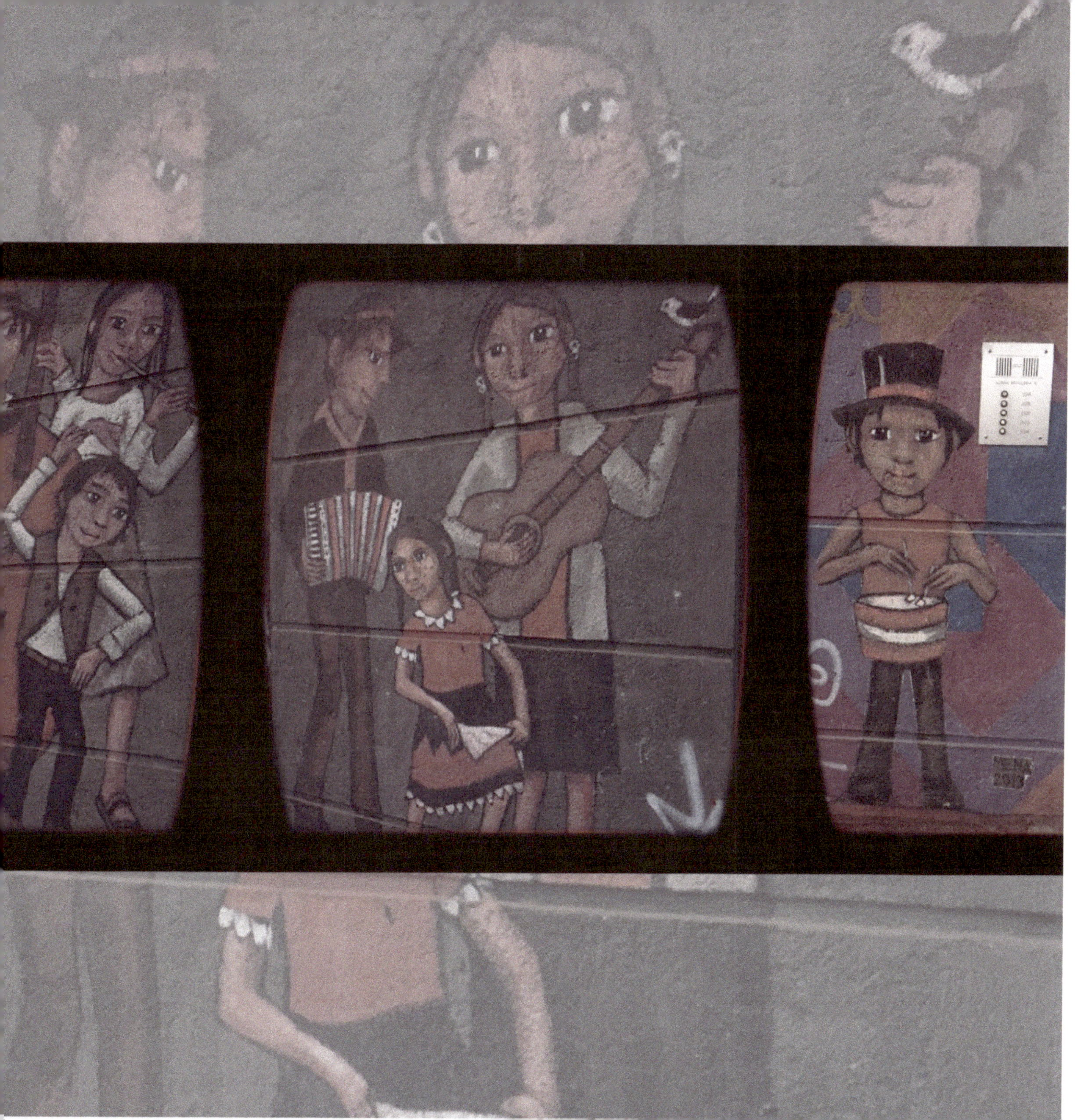

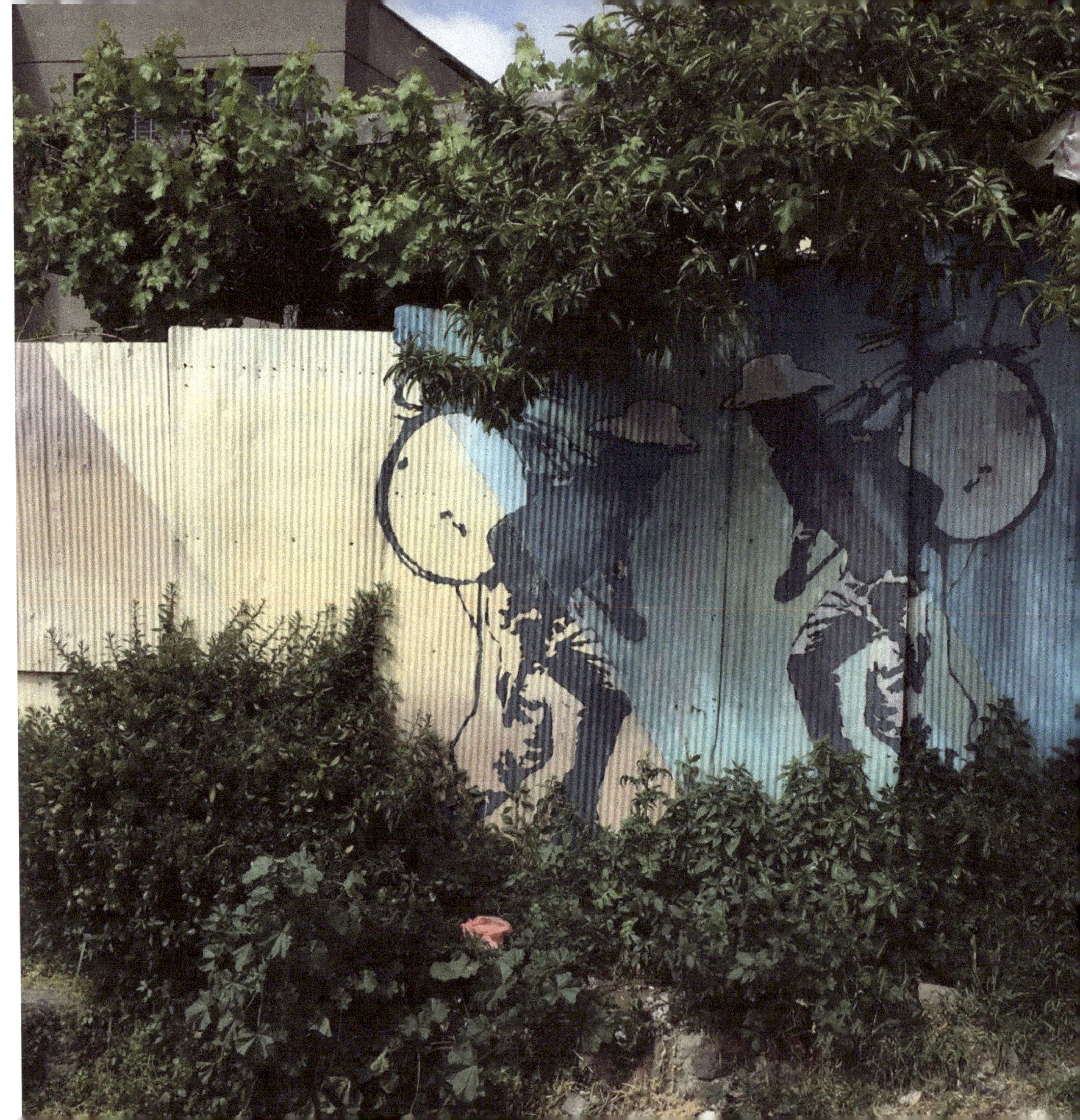

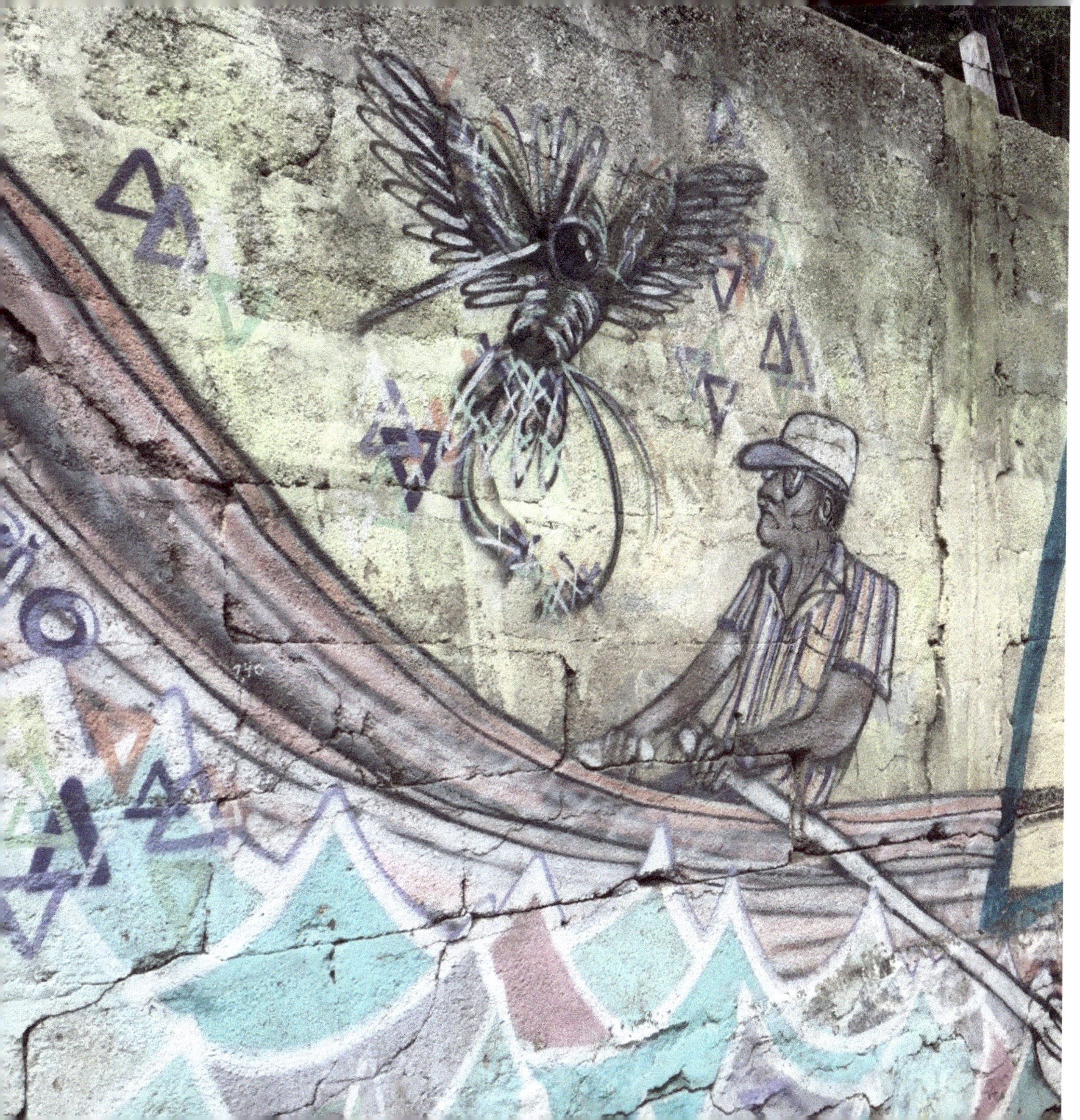

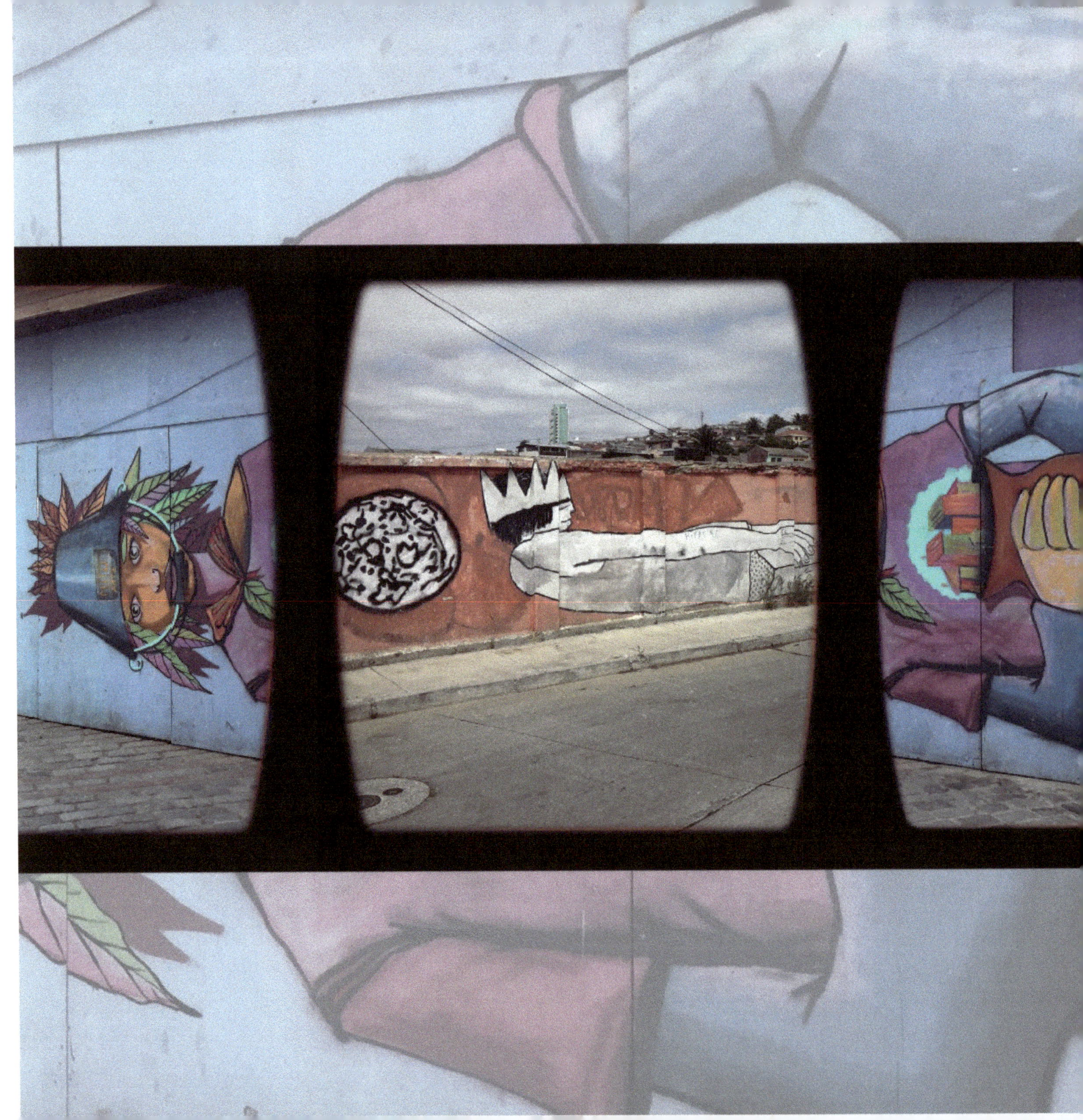

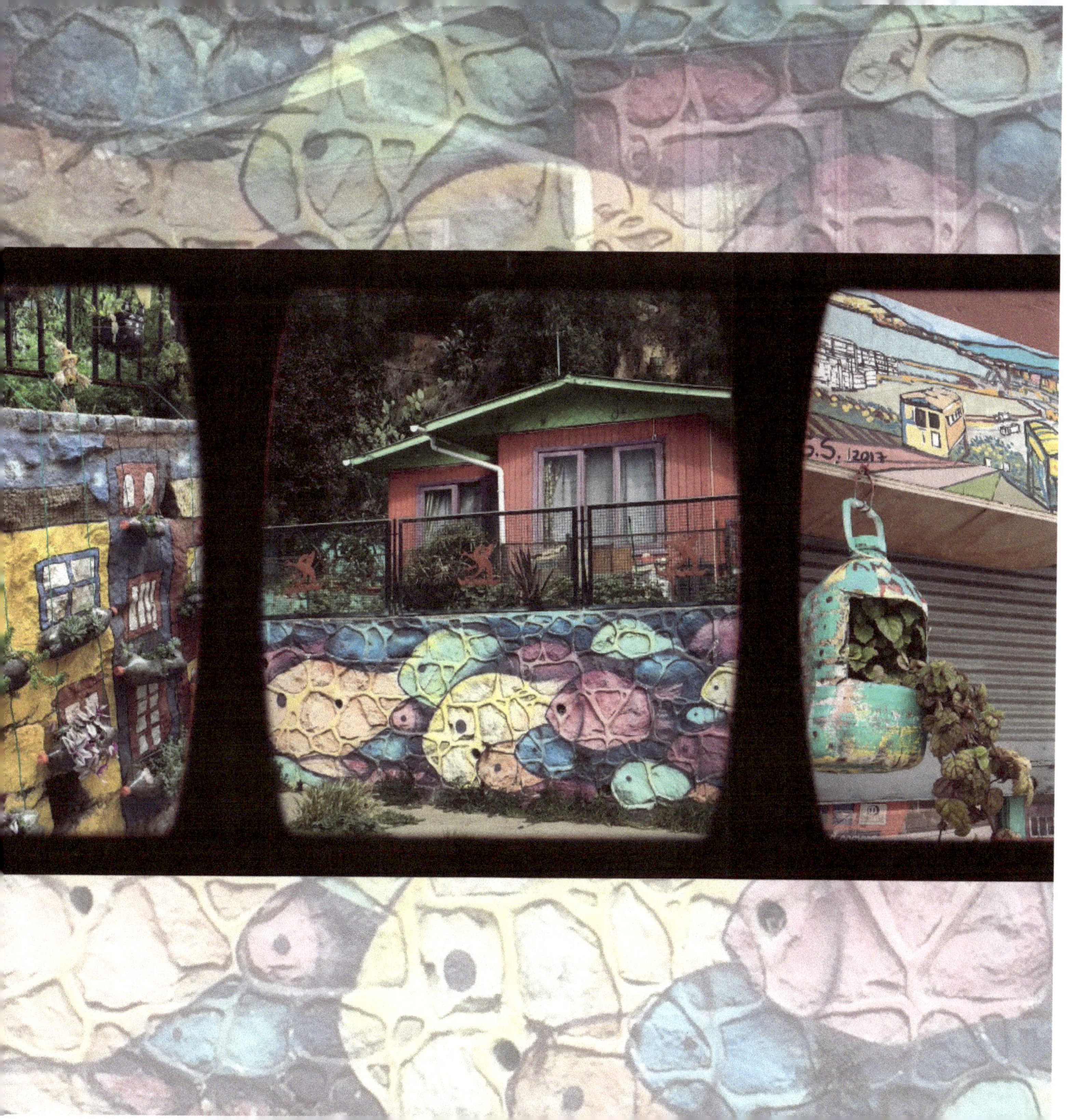

S.S. 2017

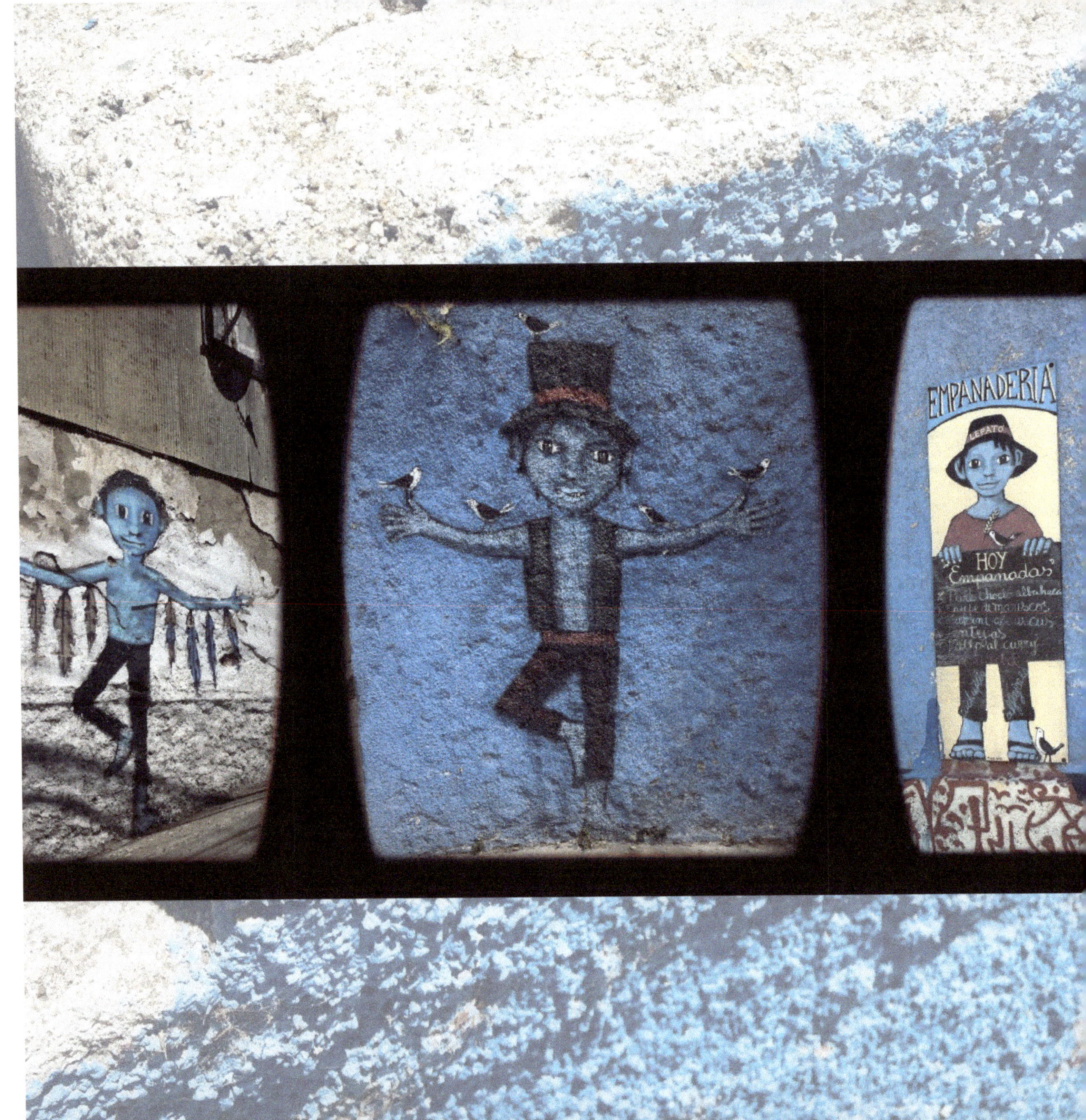
EMPANADERIA
LEPATO
HOY
Empanadas'

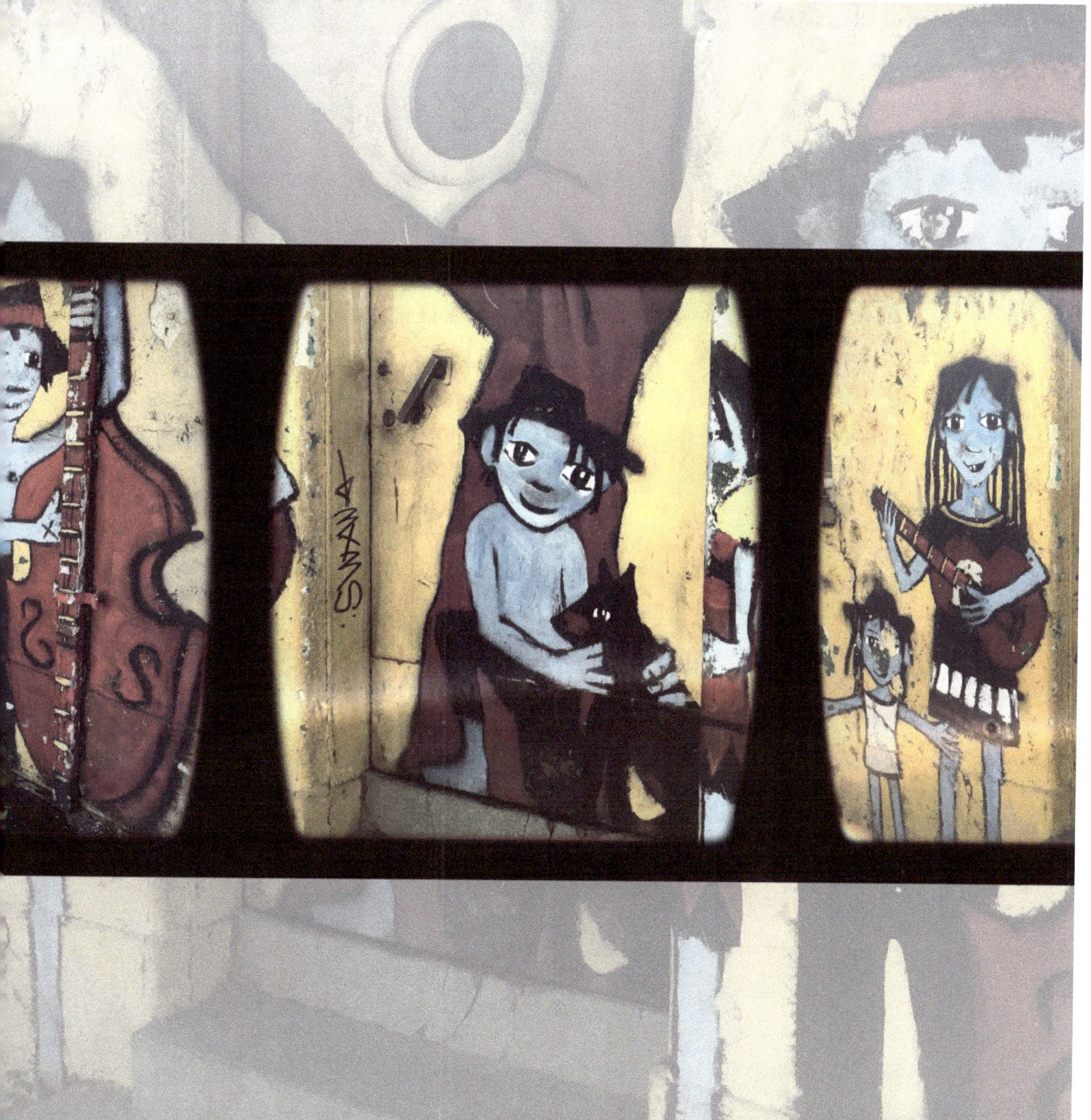

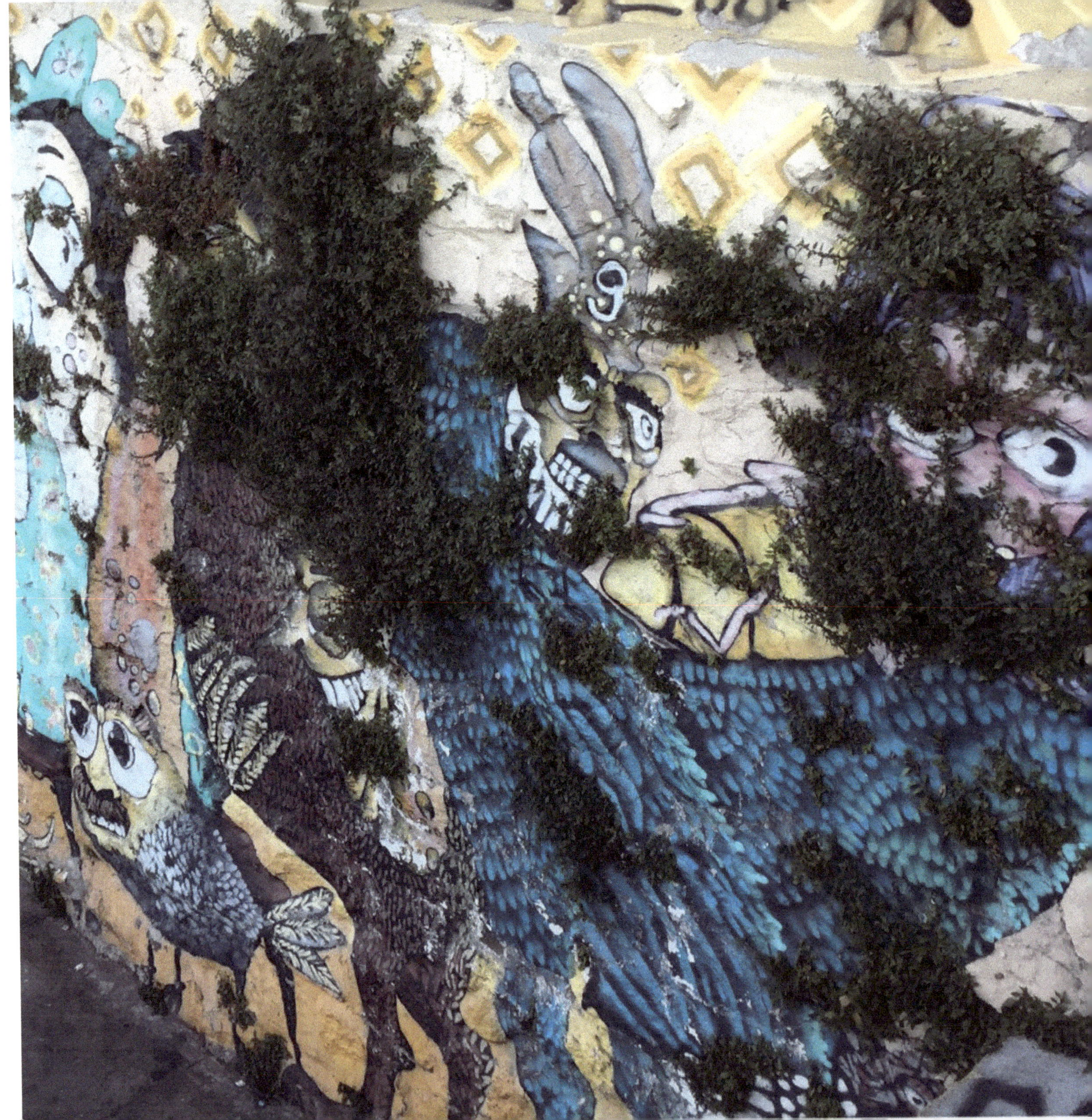

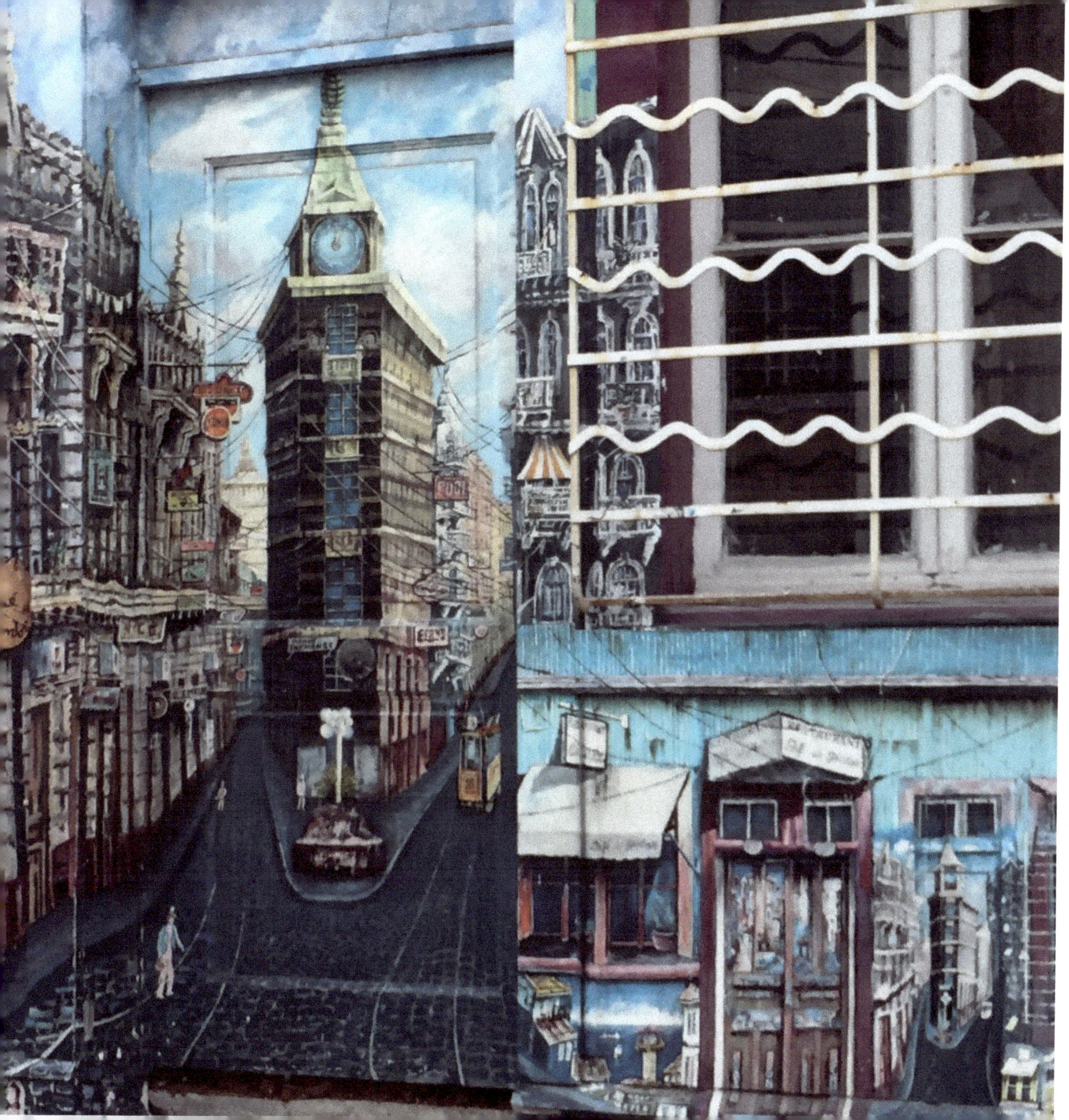

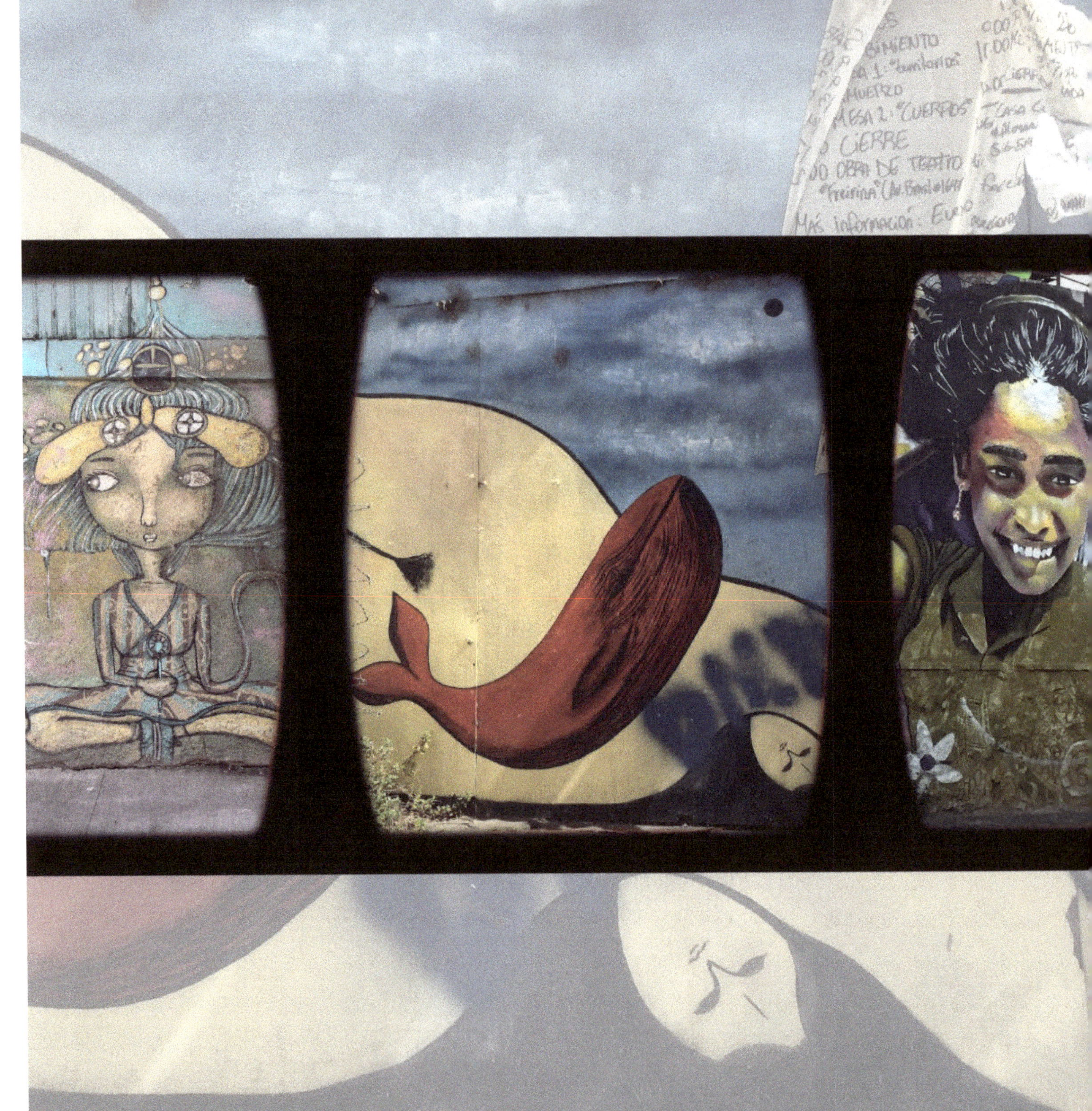

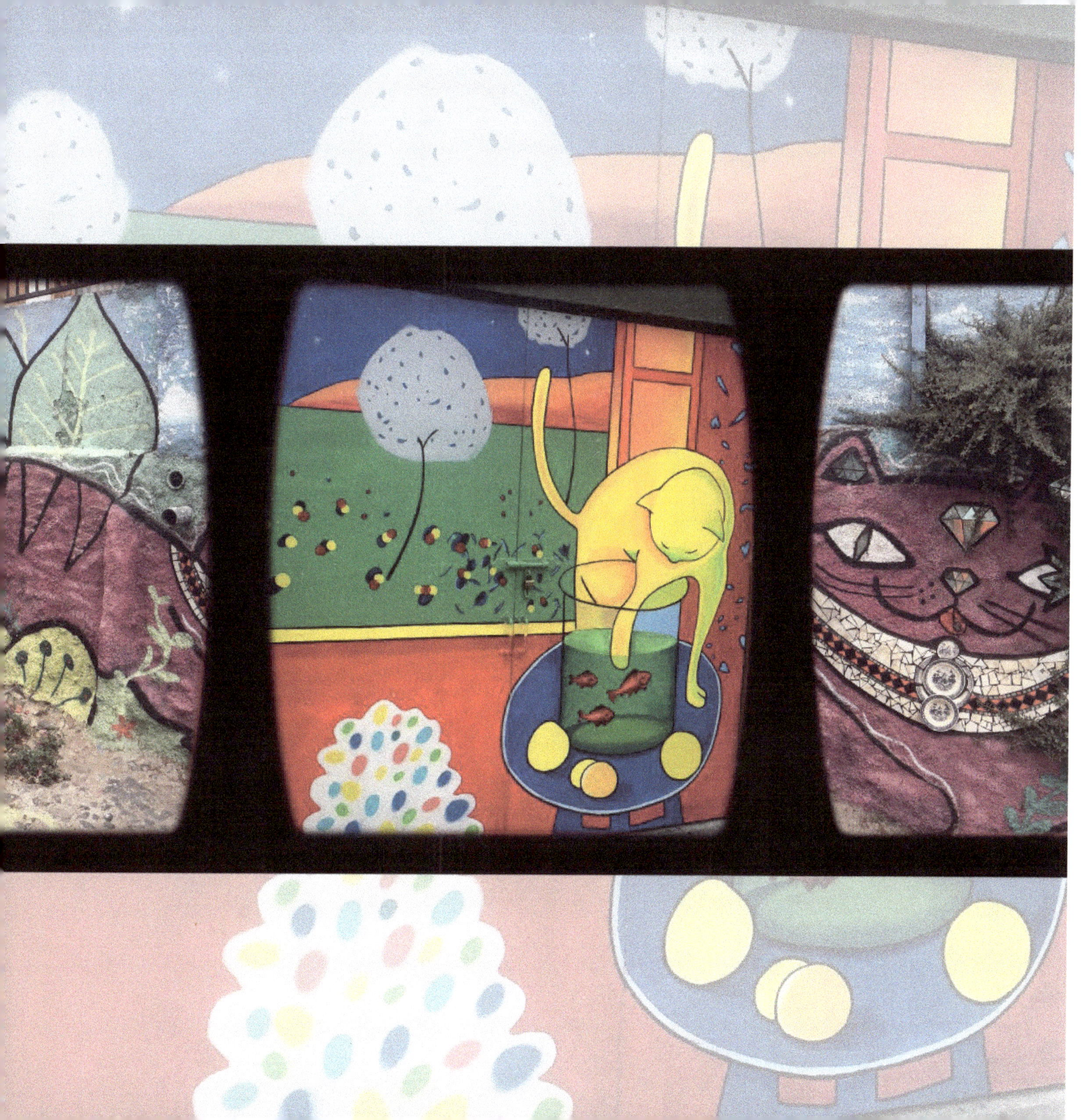

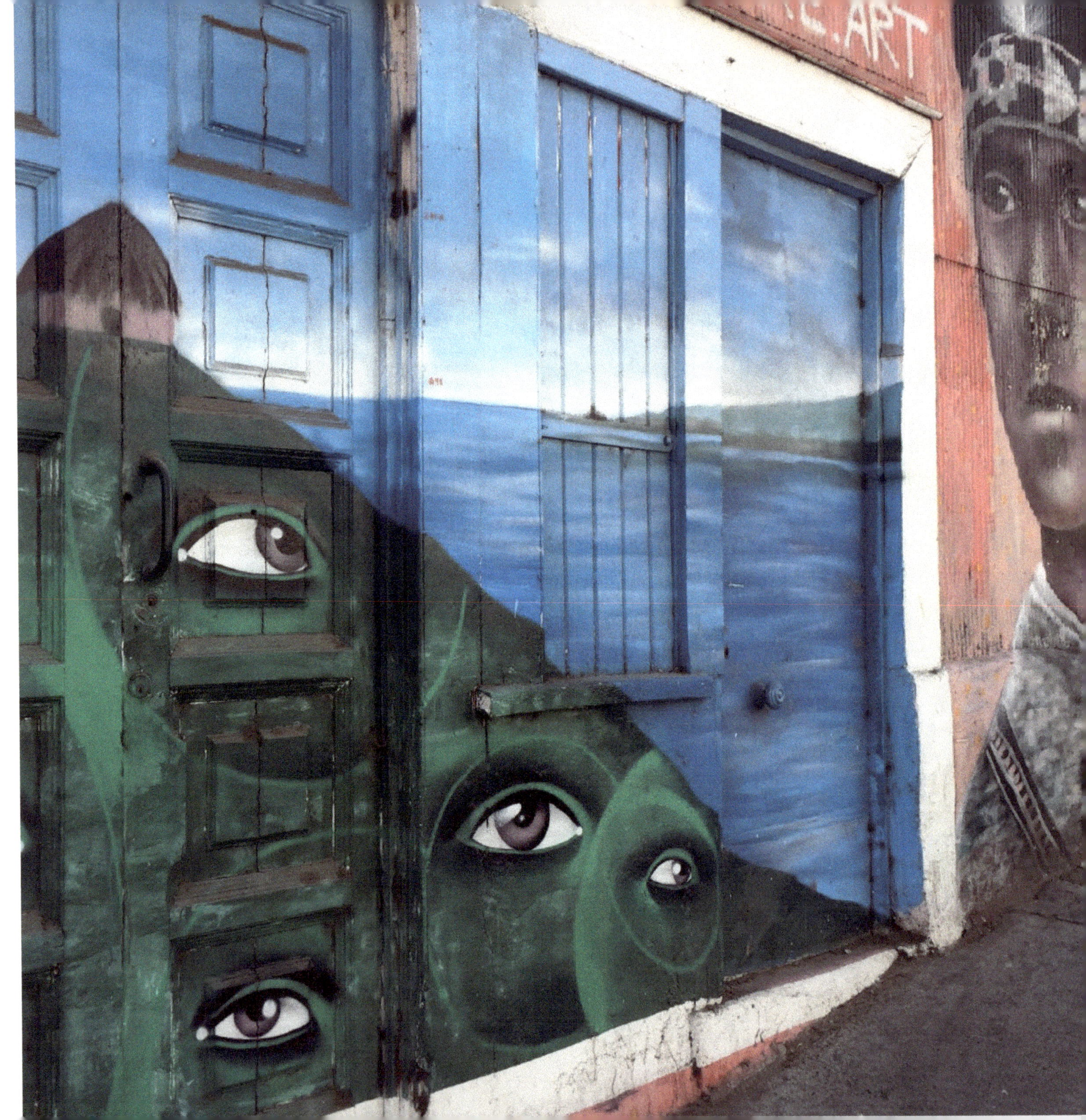
.ART

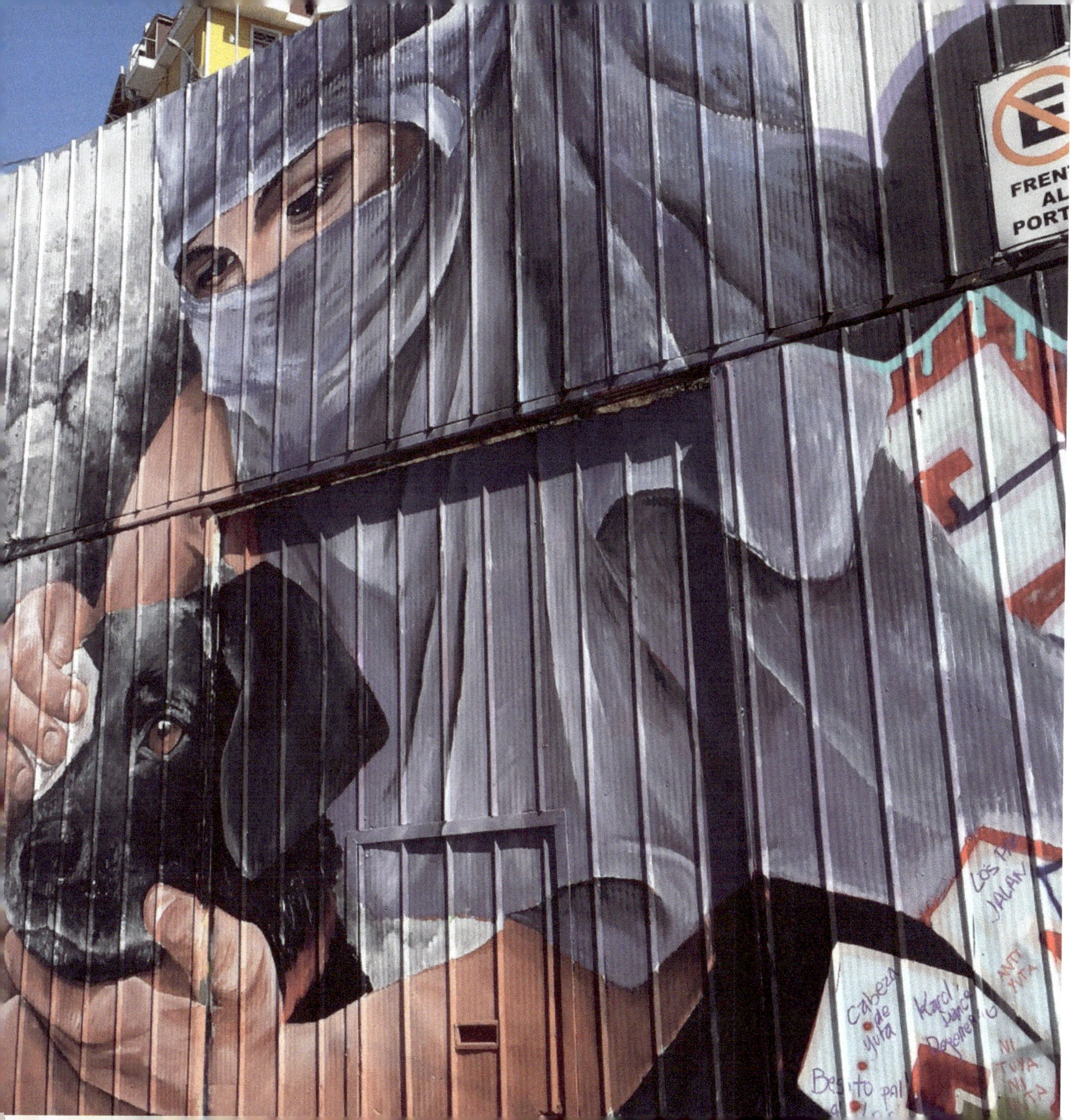
FRENT
AL
PORT
Cabeza
de
yuta
Karol
Beso to pa
Los P
JALAN

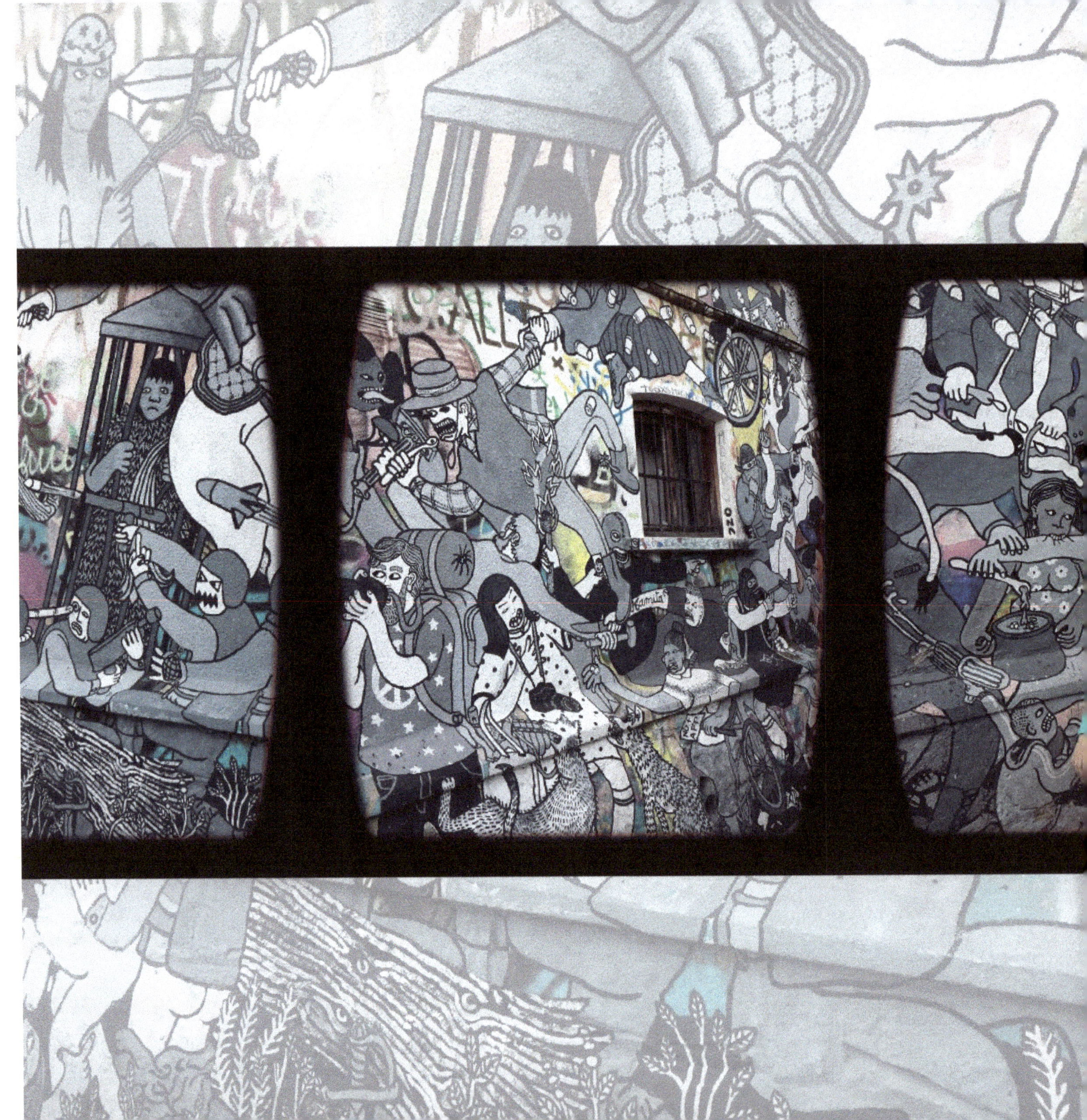

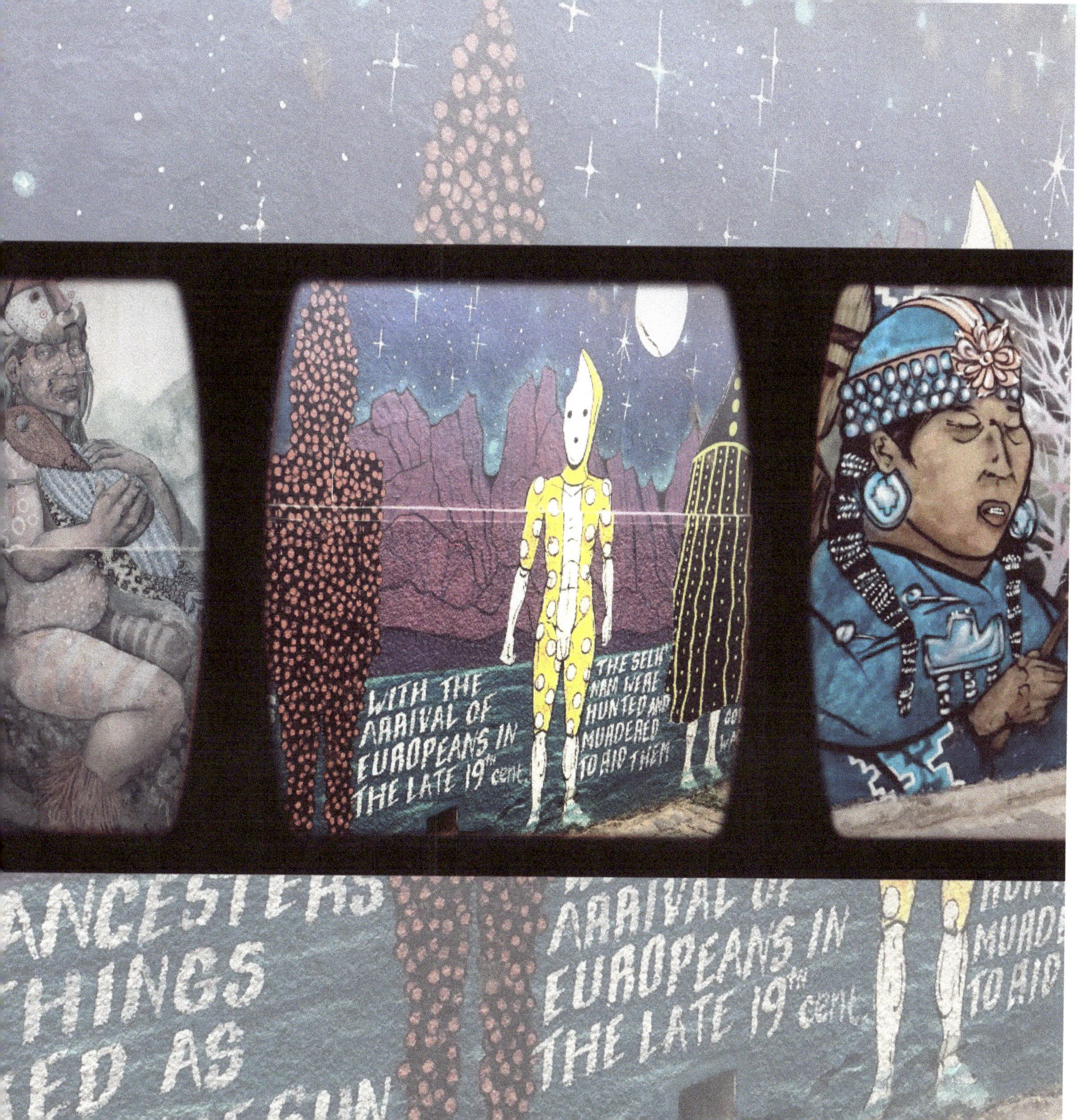

WITH THE ARRIVAL OF EUROPEANS IN THE LATE 19th cent.
THE SELK NAM WERE HUNTED AND MURDERED TO AID THEM
ANCESTERS
THINGS
ED AS
ARRIVAL OF EUROPEANS IN THE LATE 19th cent.
MURDE
TO AID

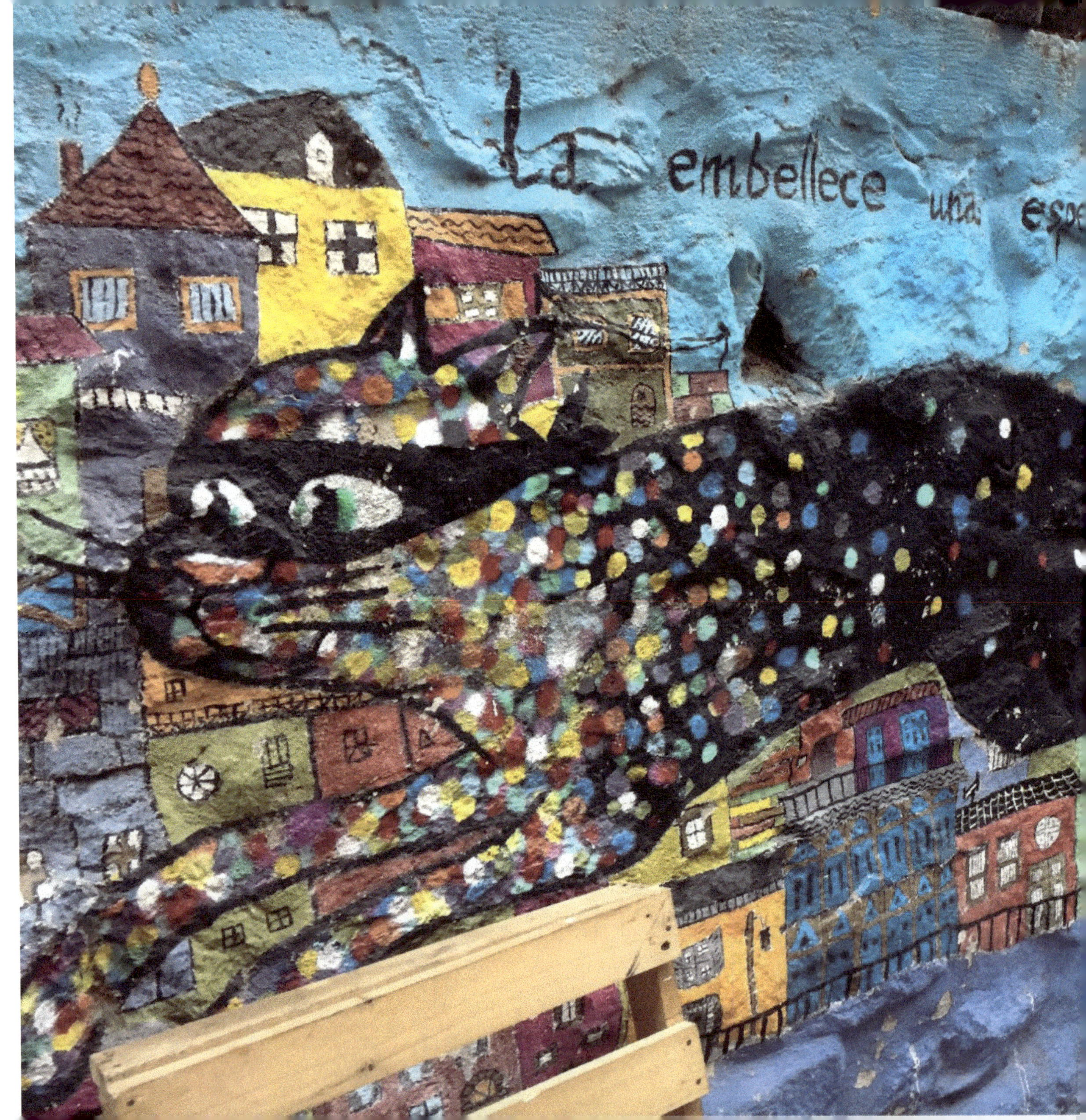
la embellece una espe

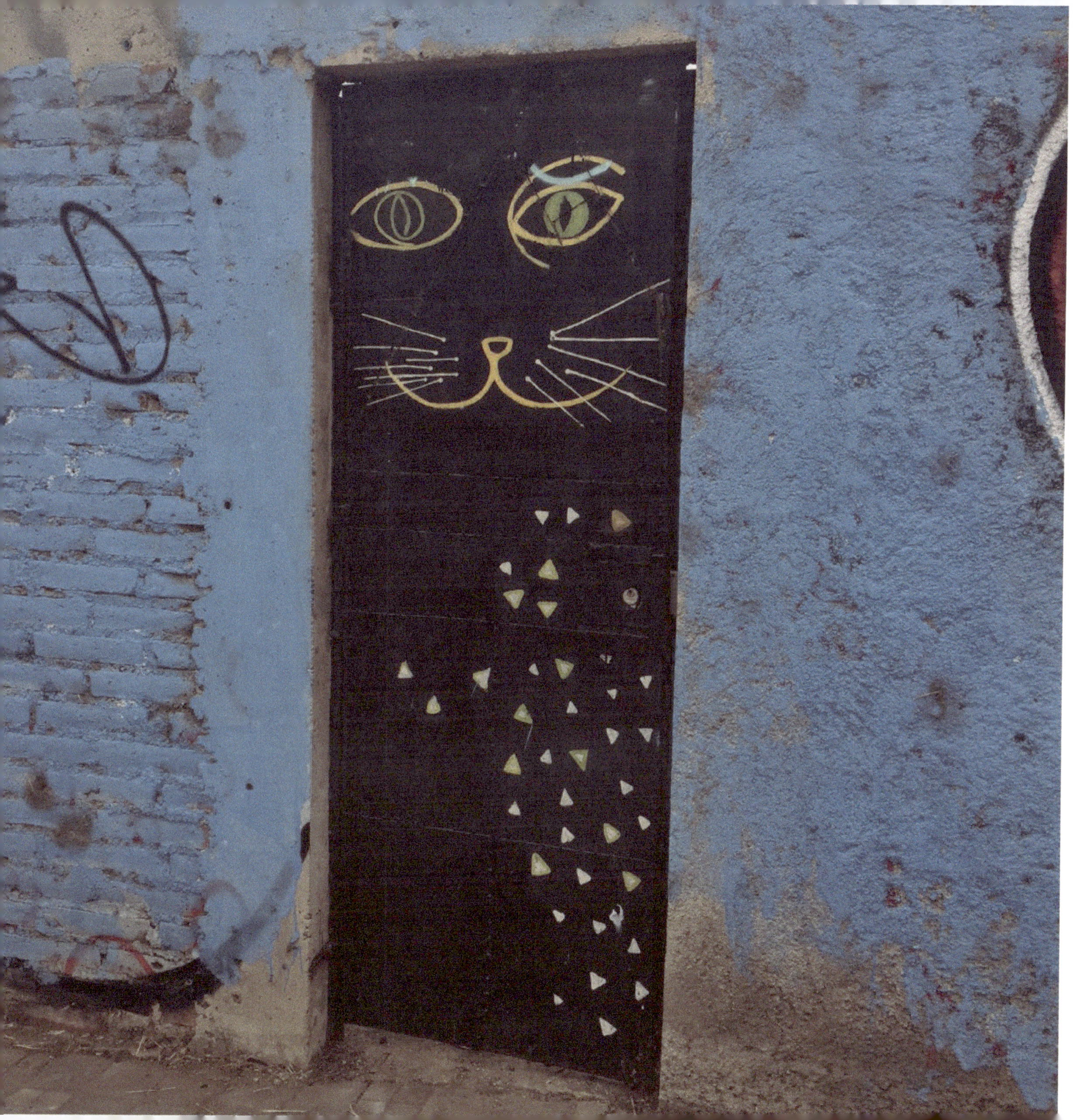

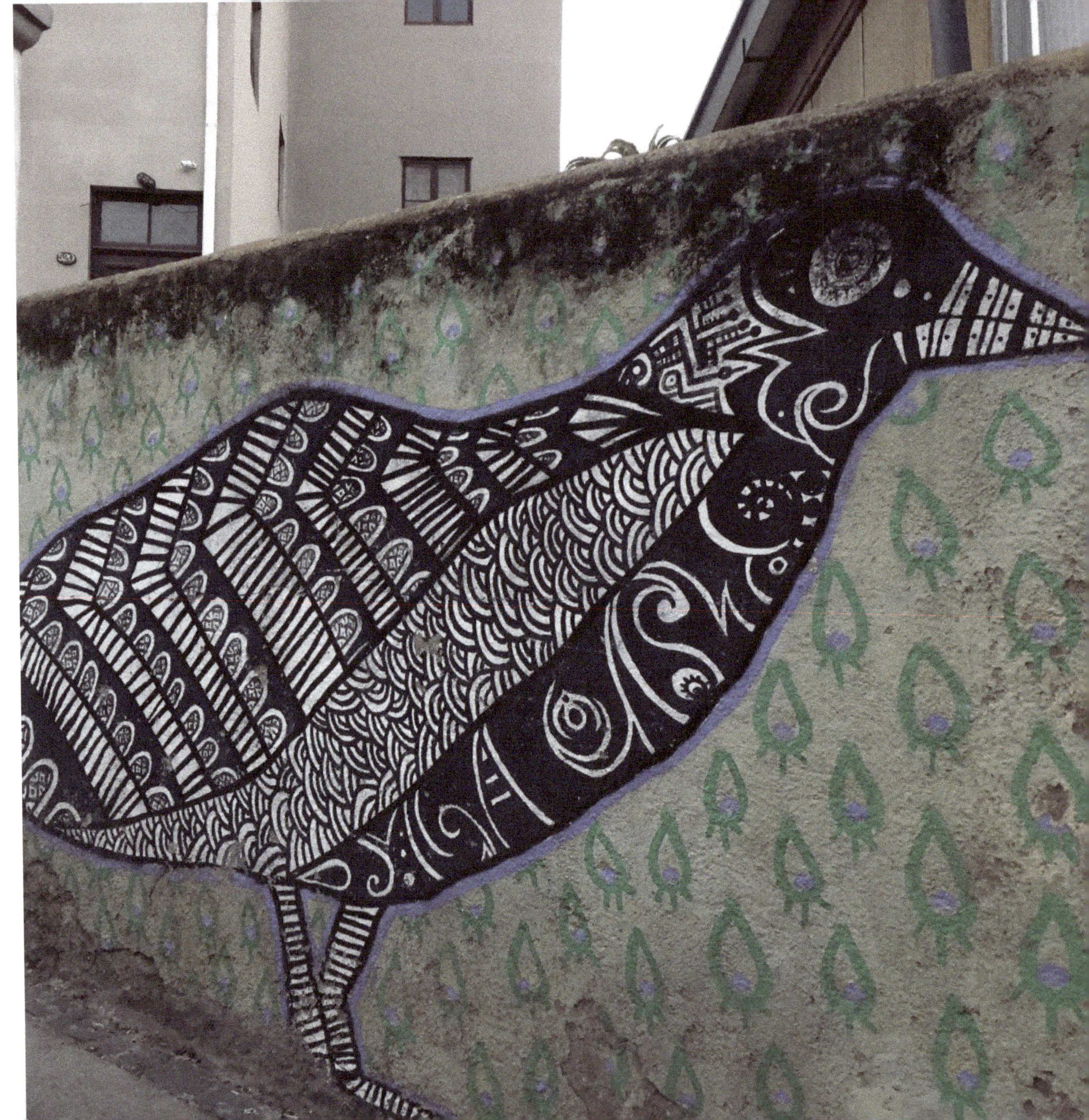

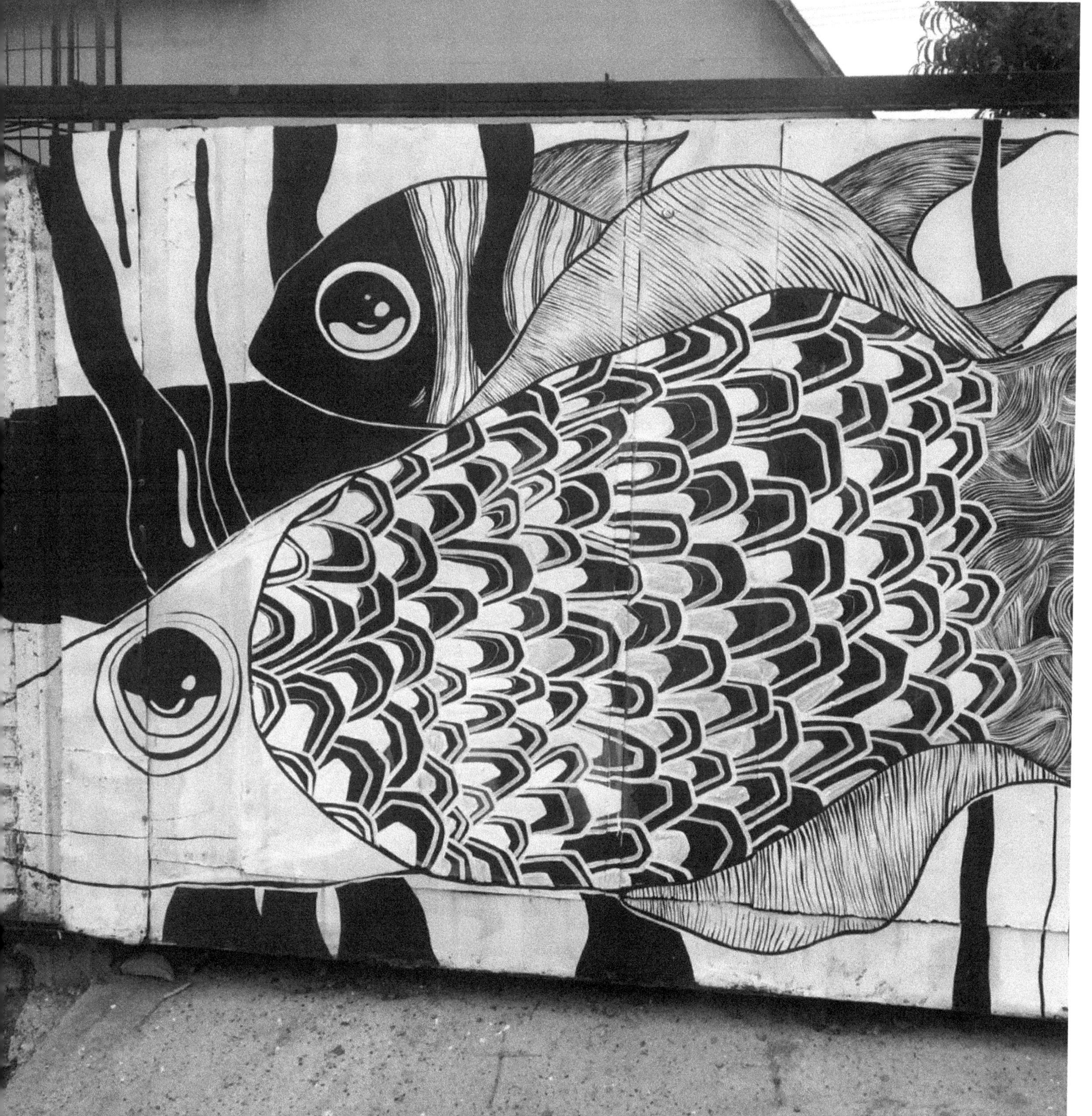

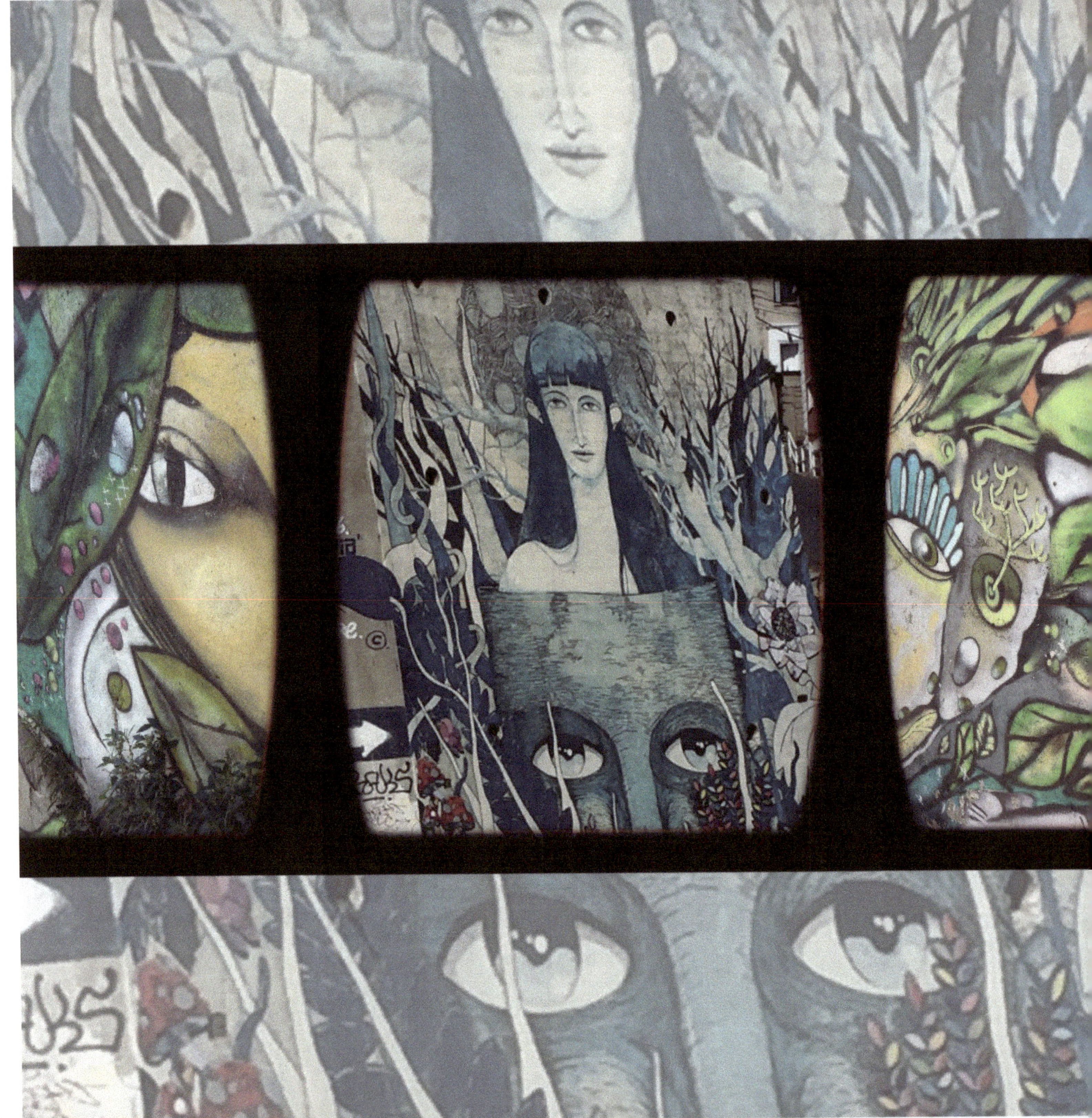

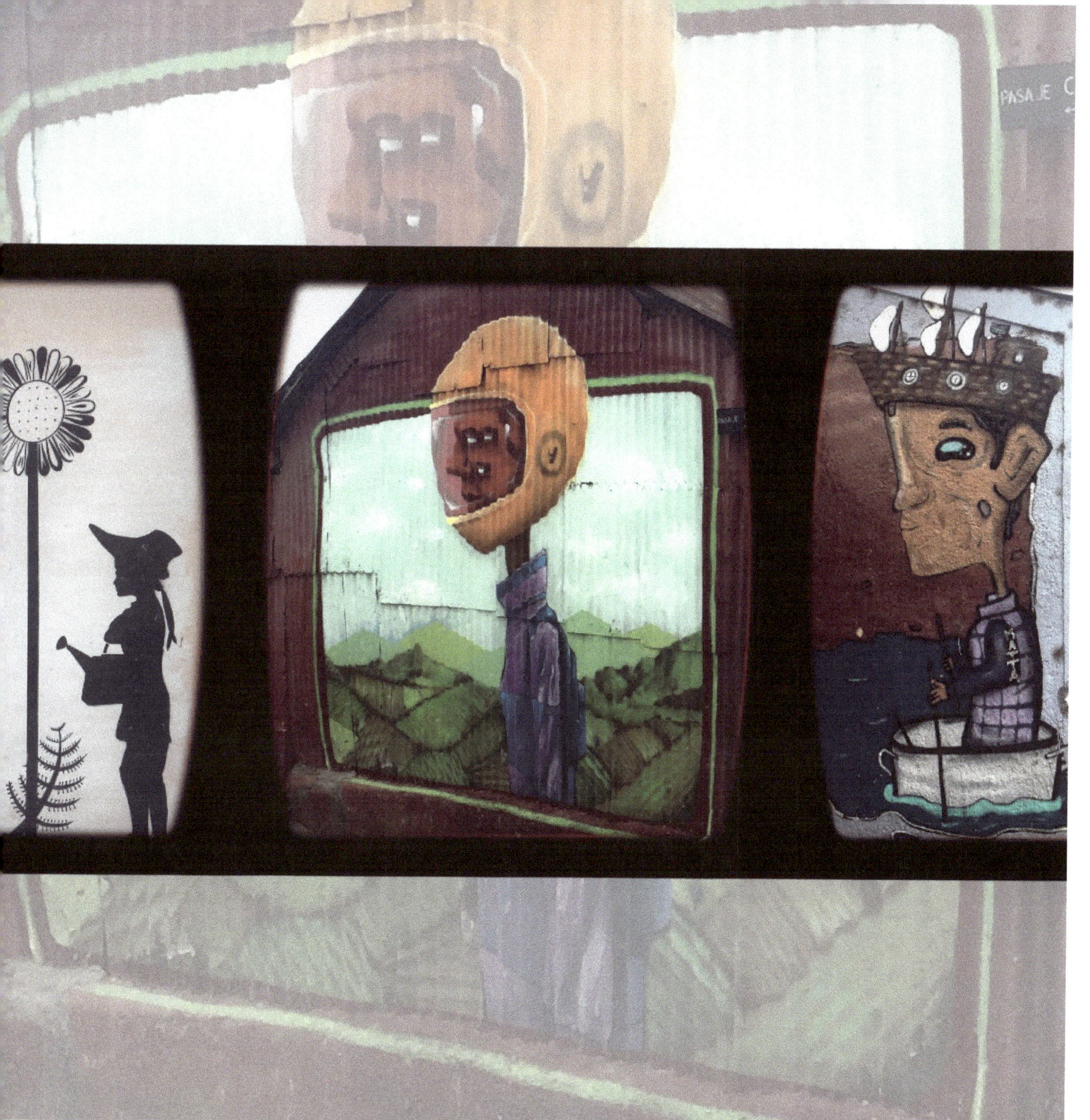
PASAJE C

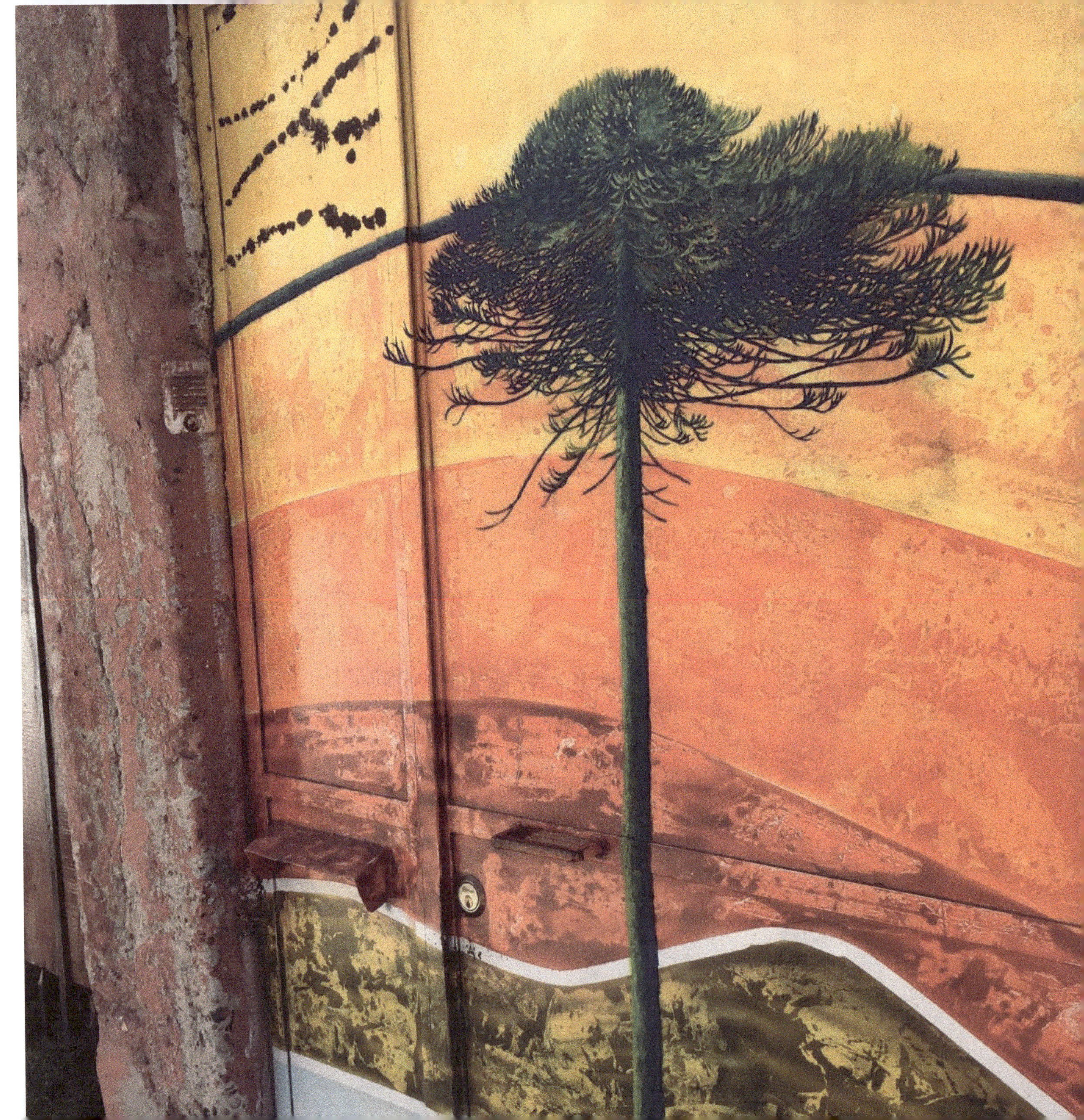

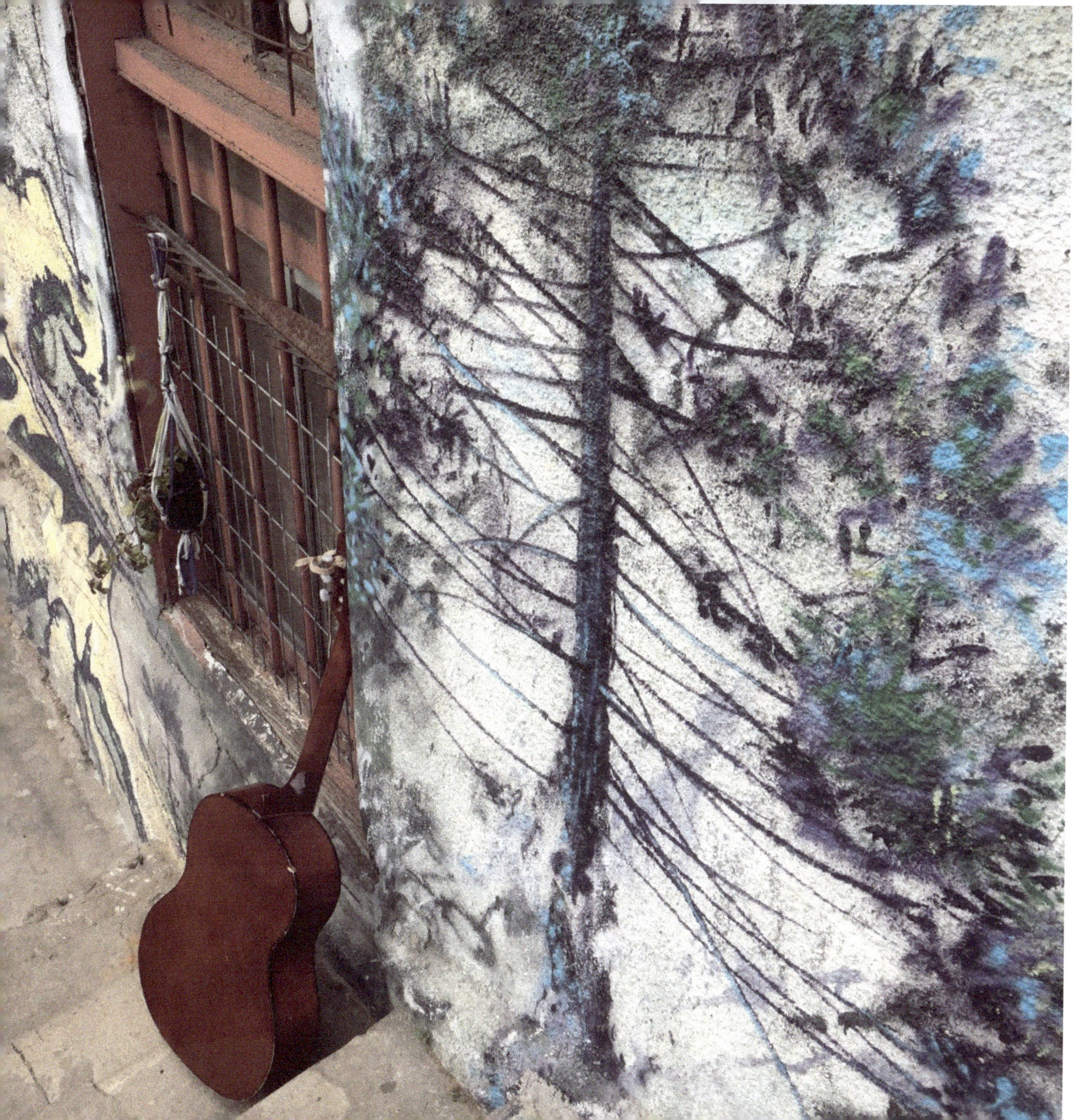

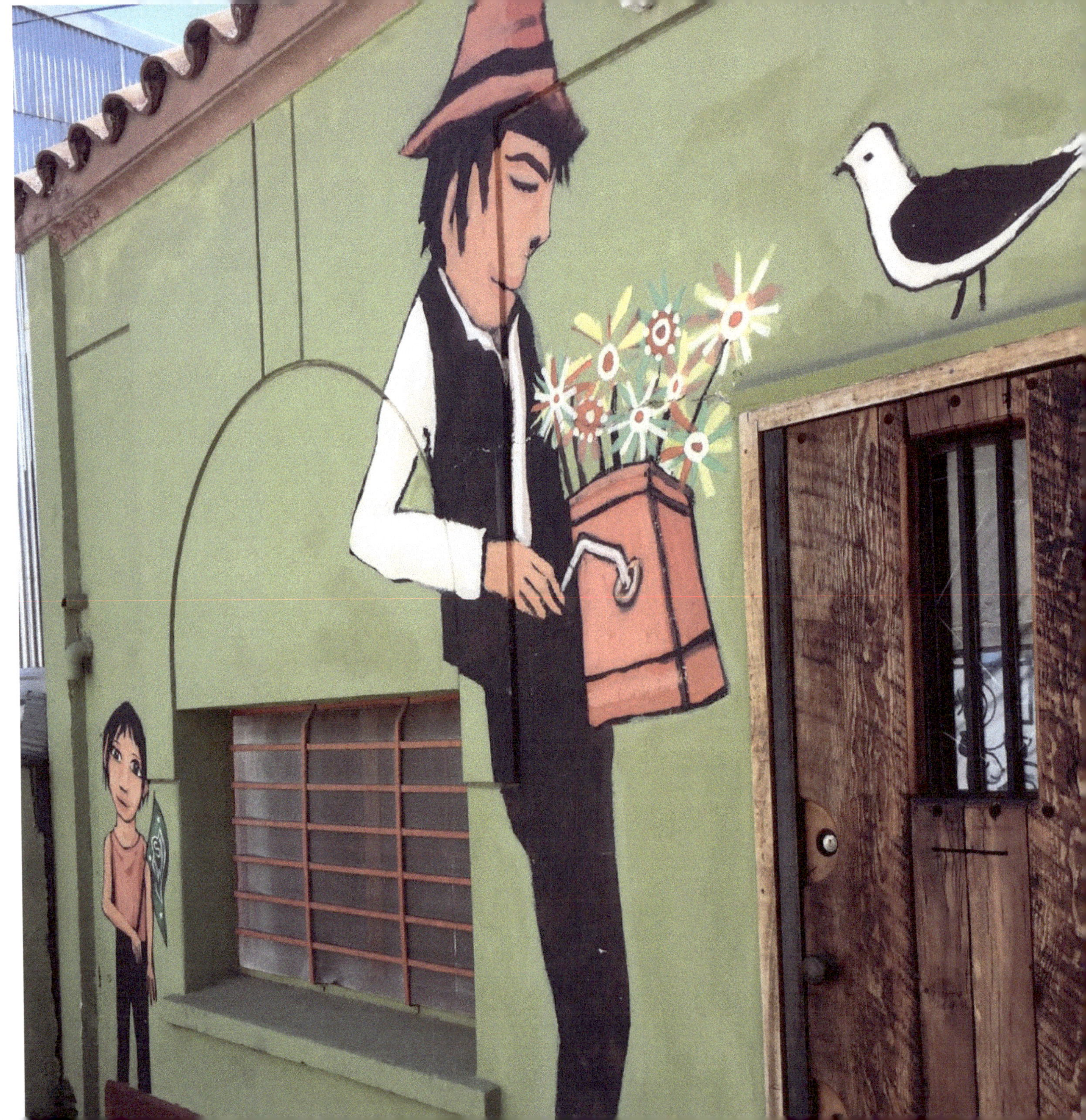

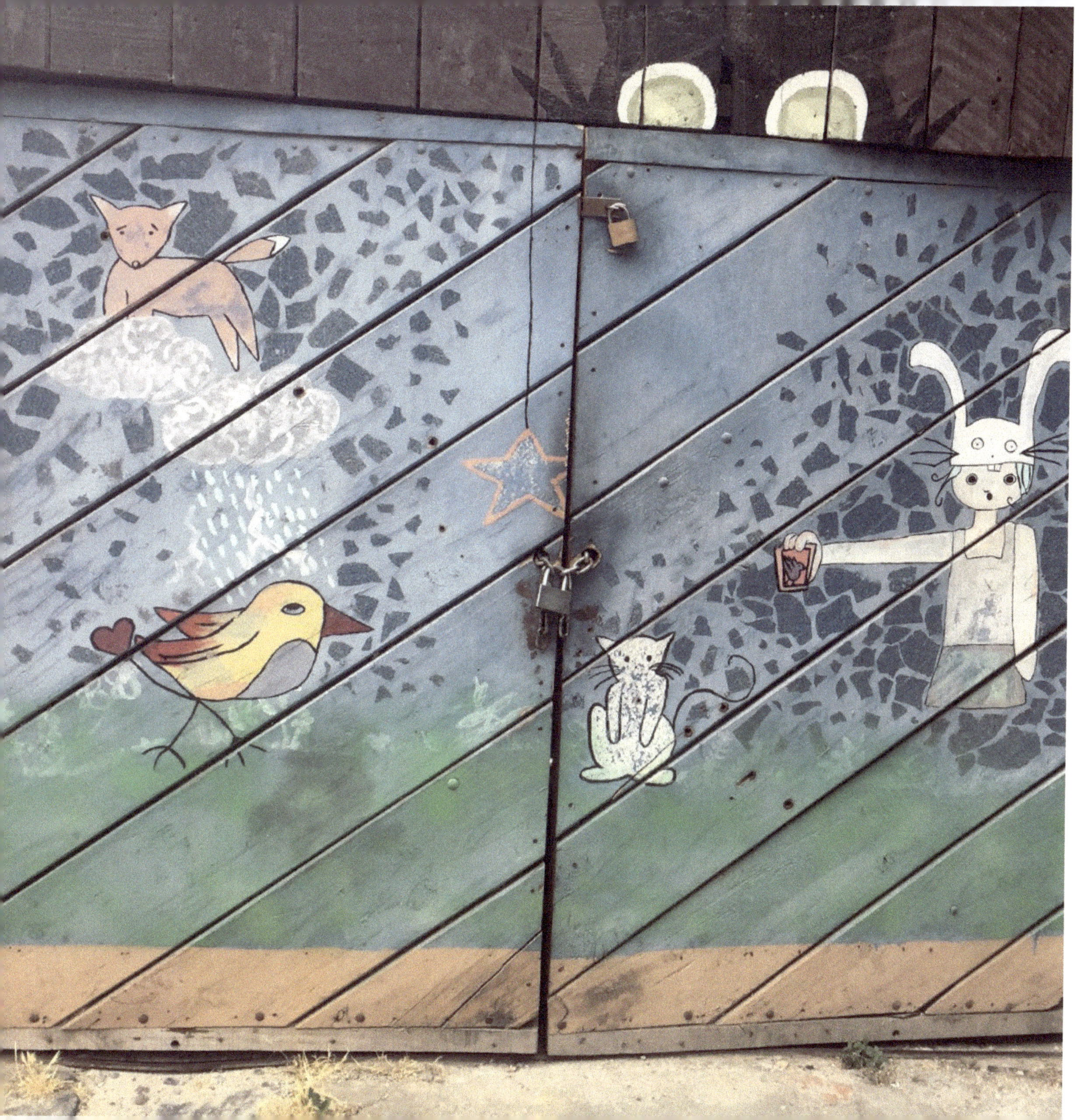

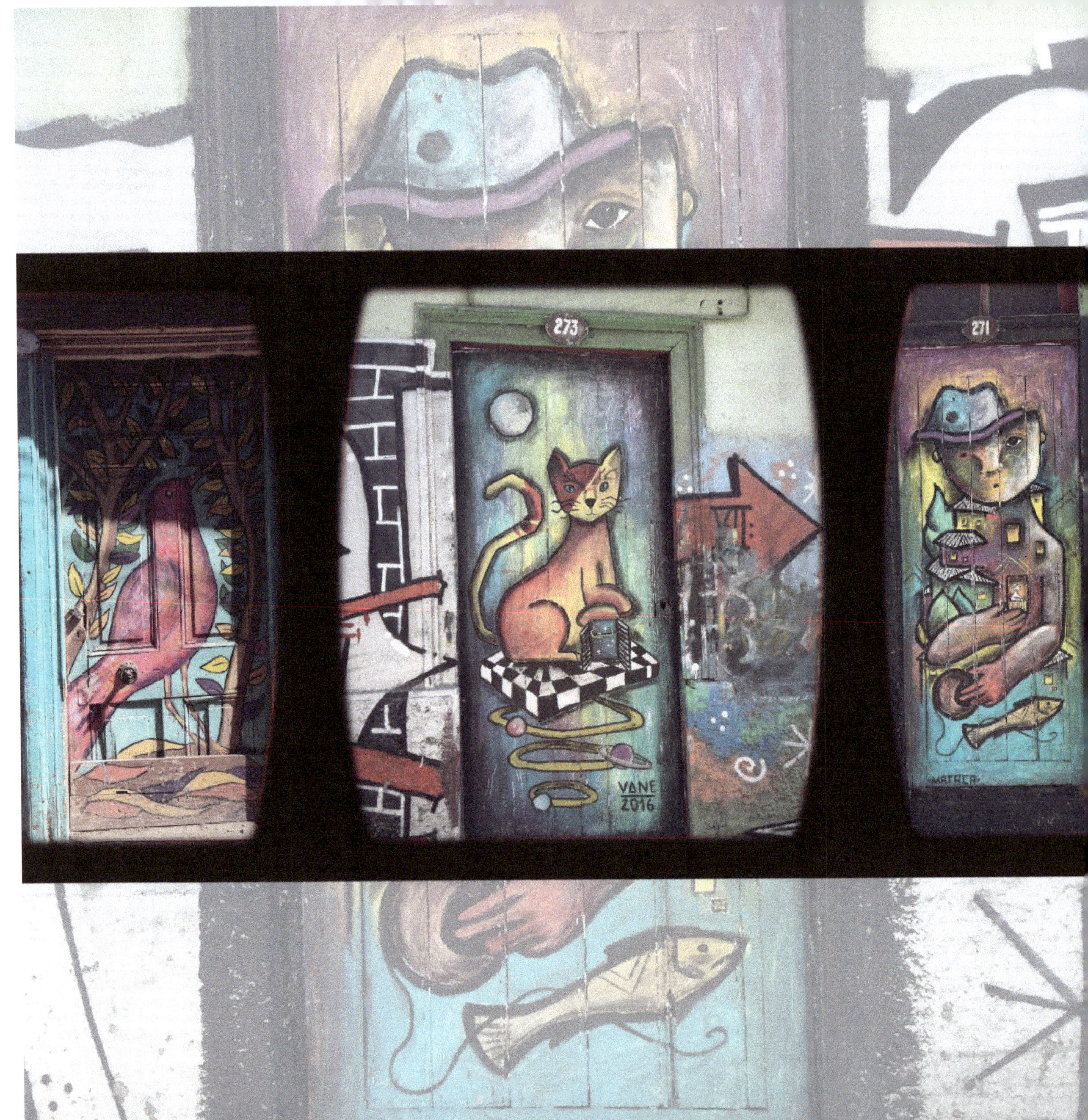
273
271
VANE
2016
MATACA

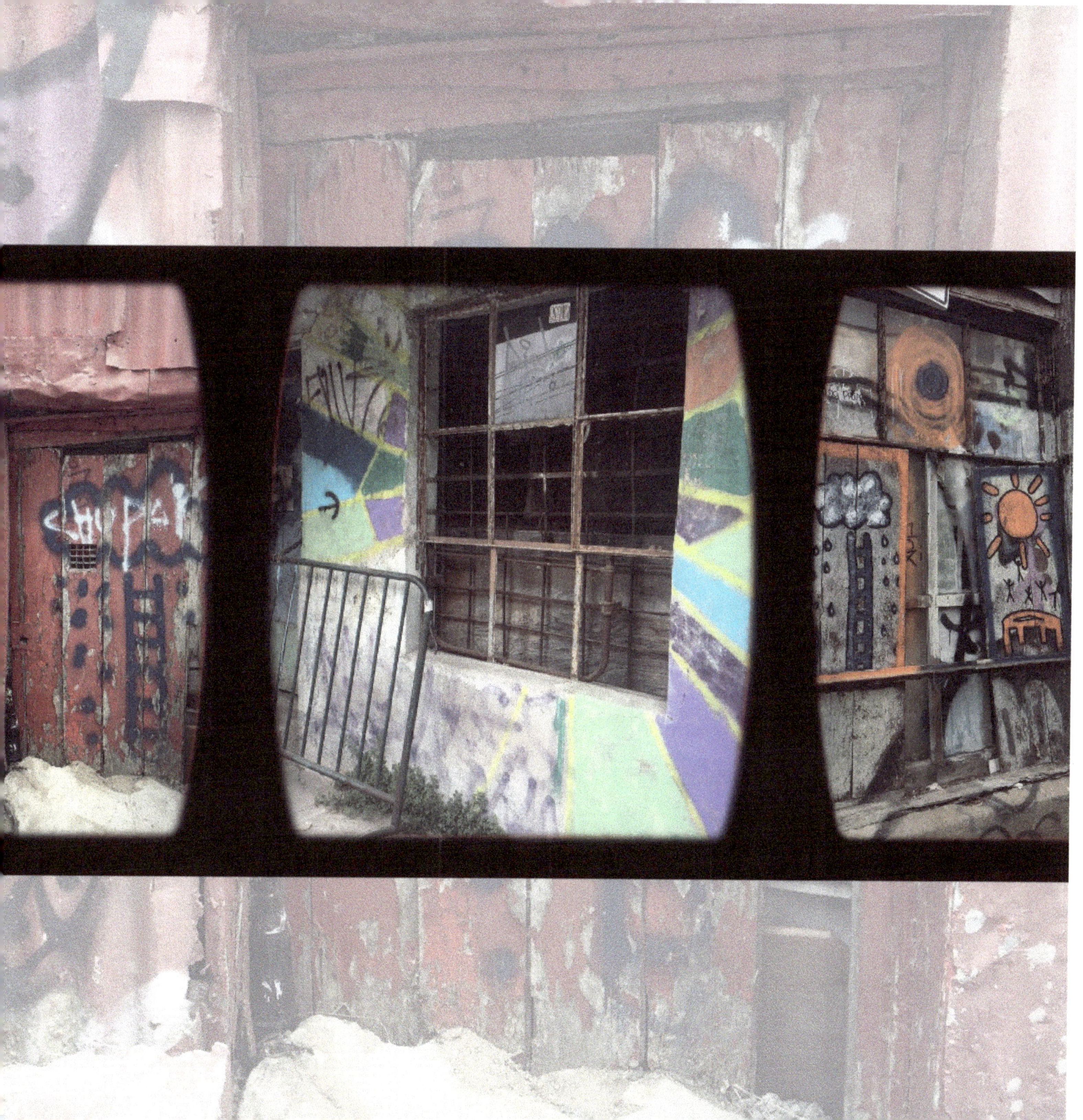

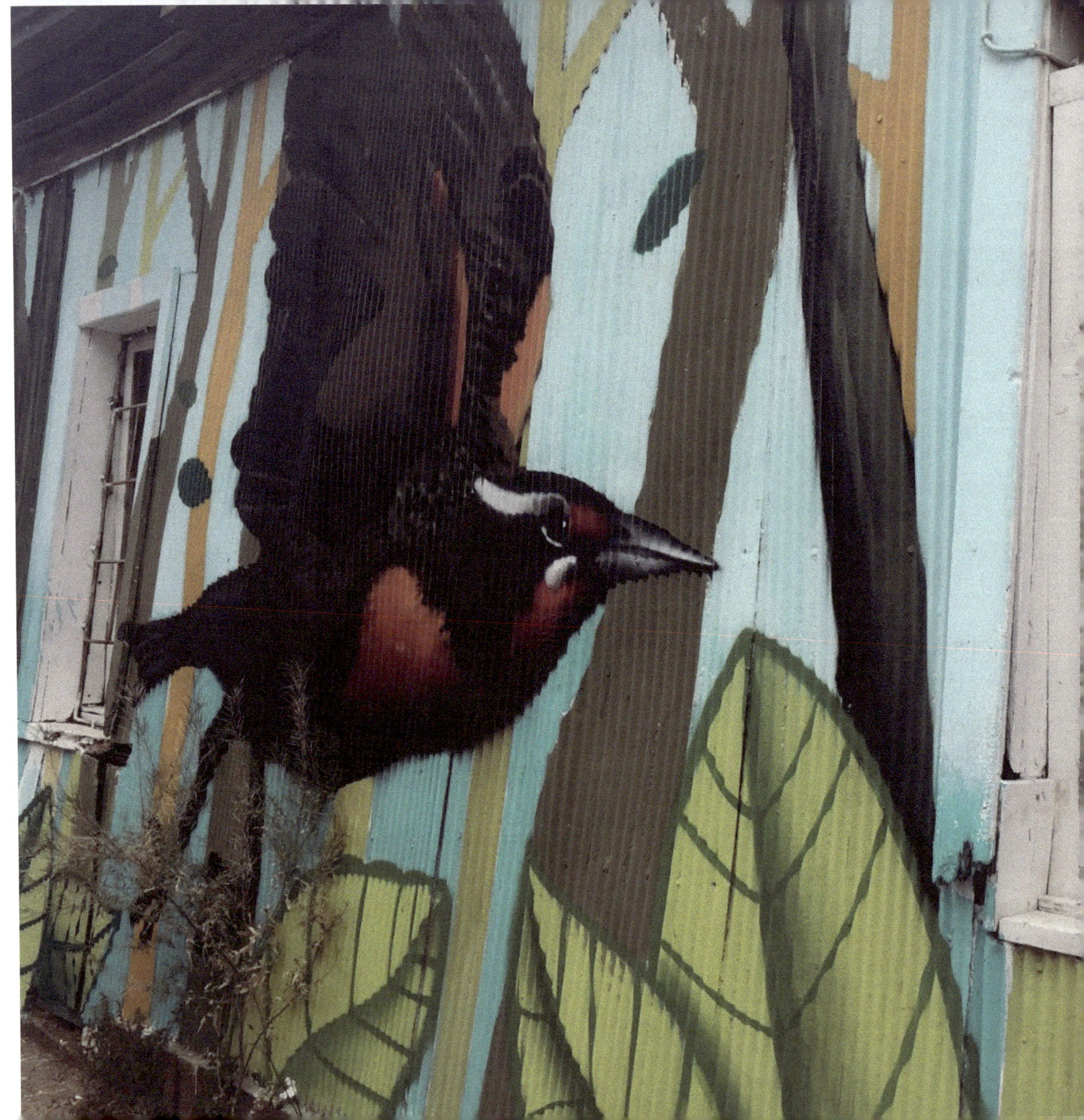

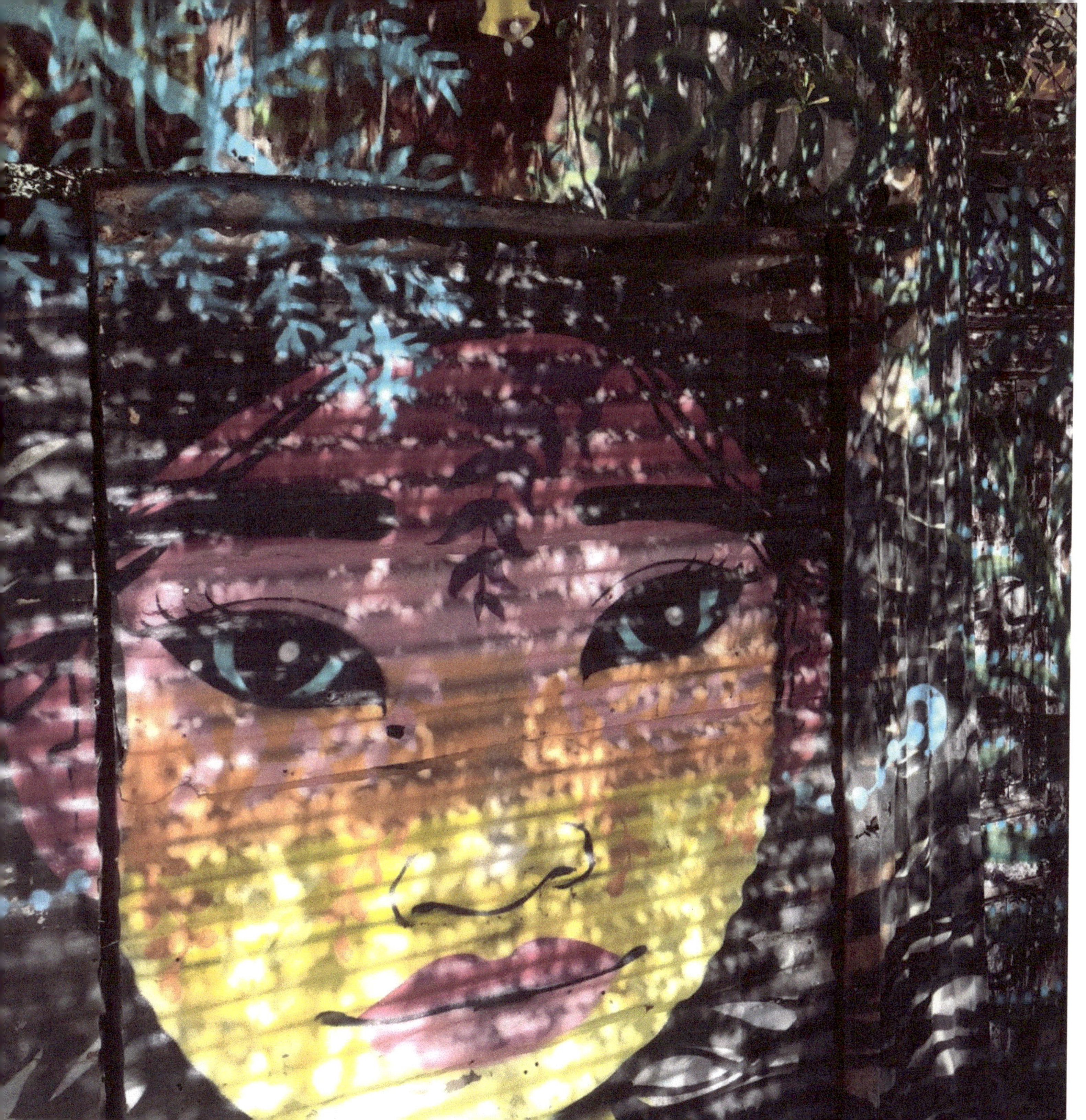

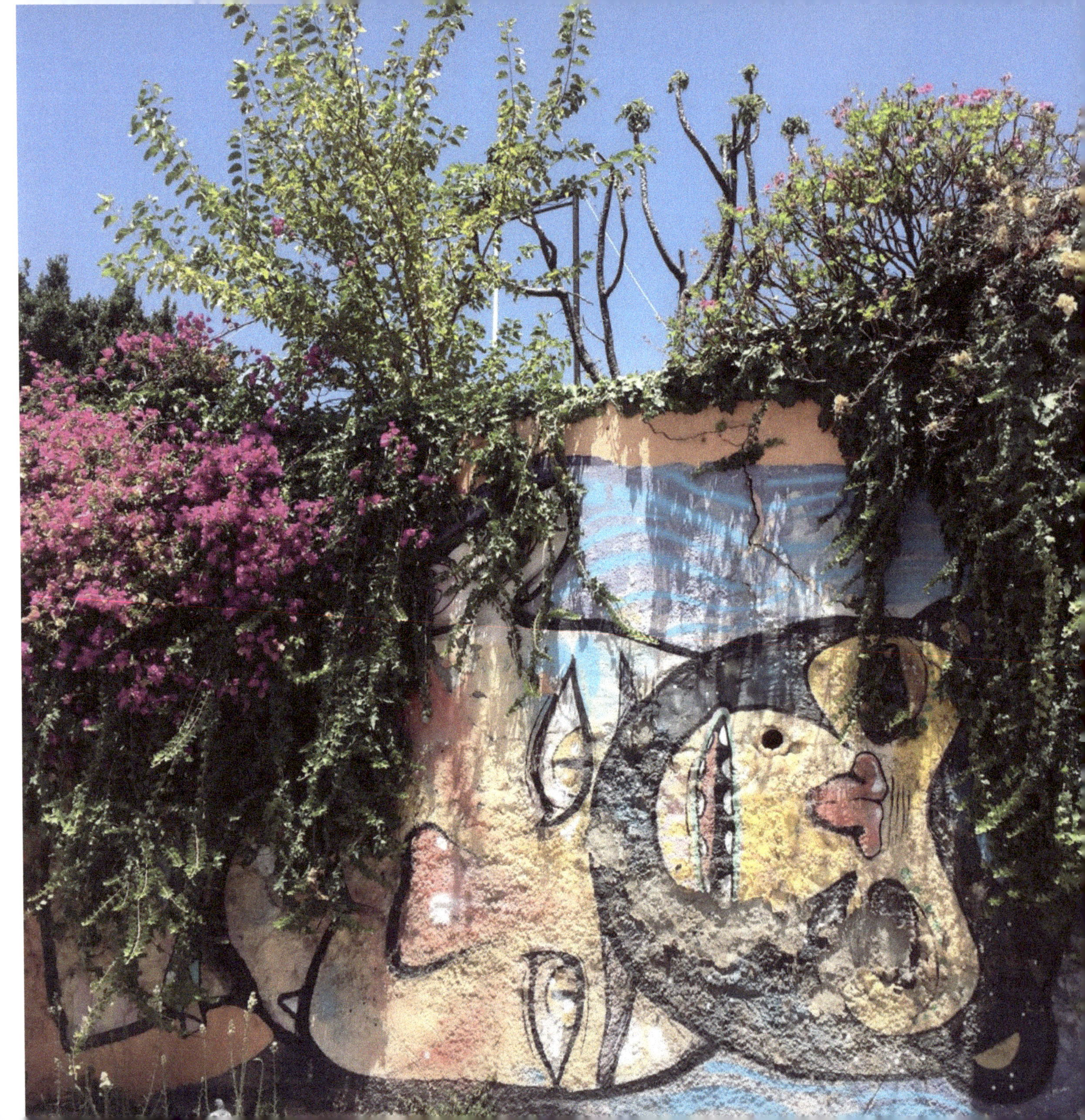

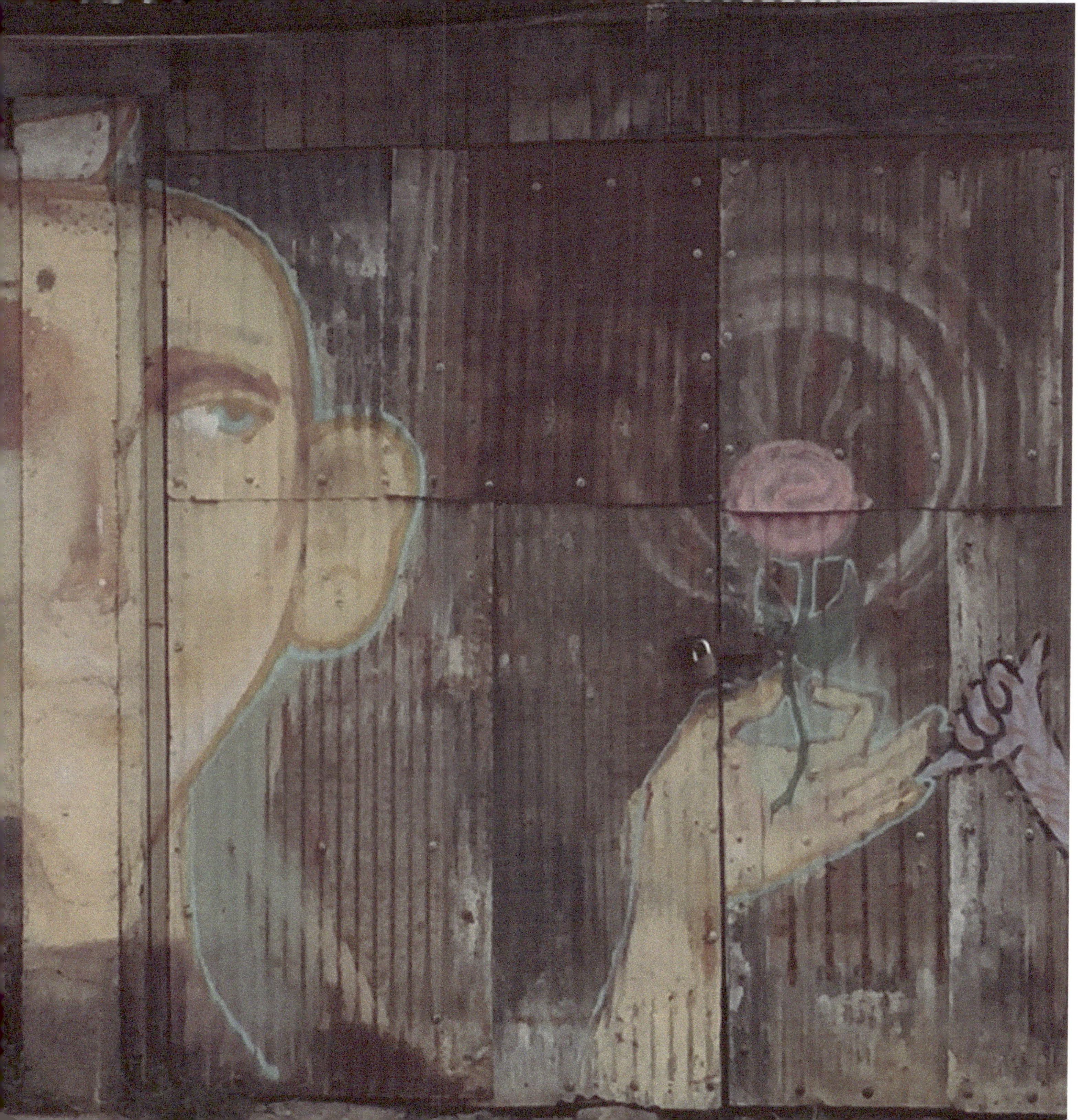

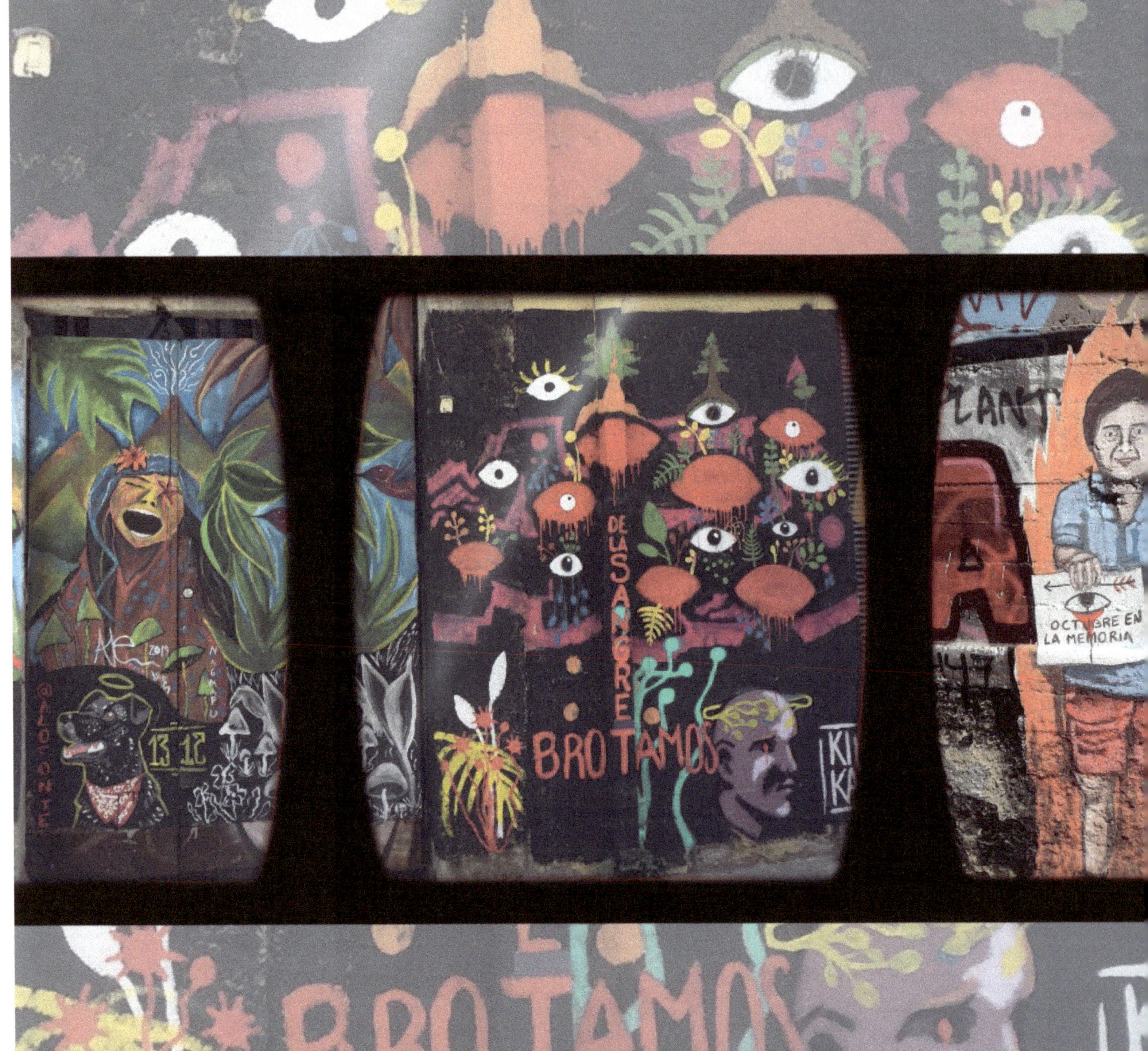

13 12
@LOS ONTE
DE LA SANGRE
BROTAMOS
KI KA
ZANT
OCTUBRE EN
LA MEMORIA
BROTAMOS

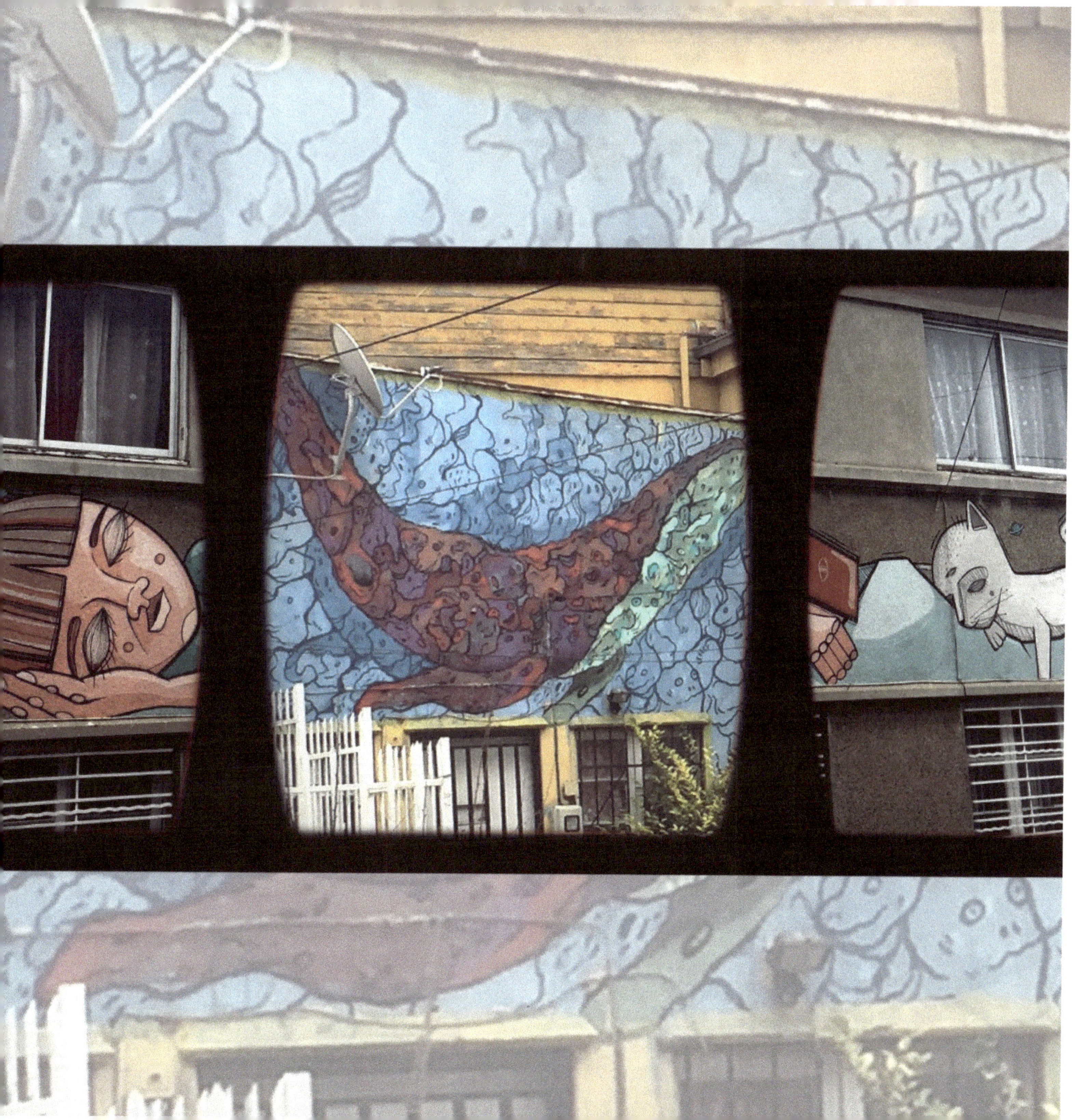

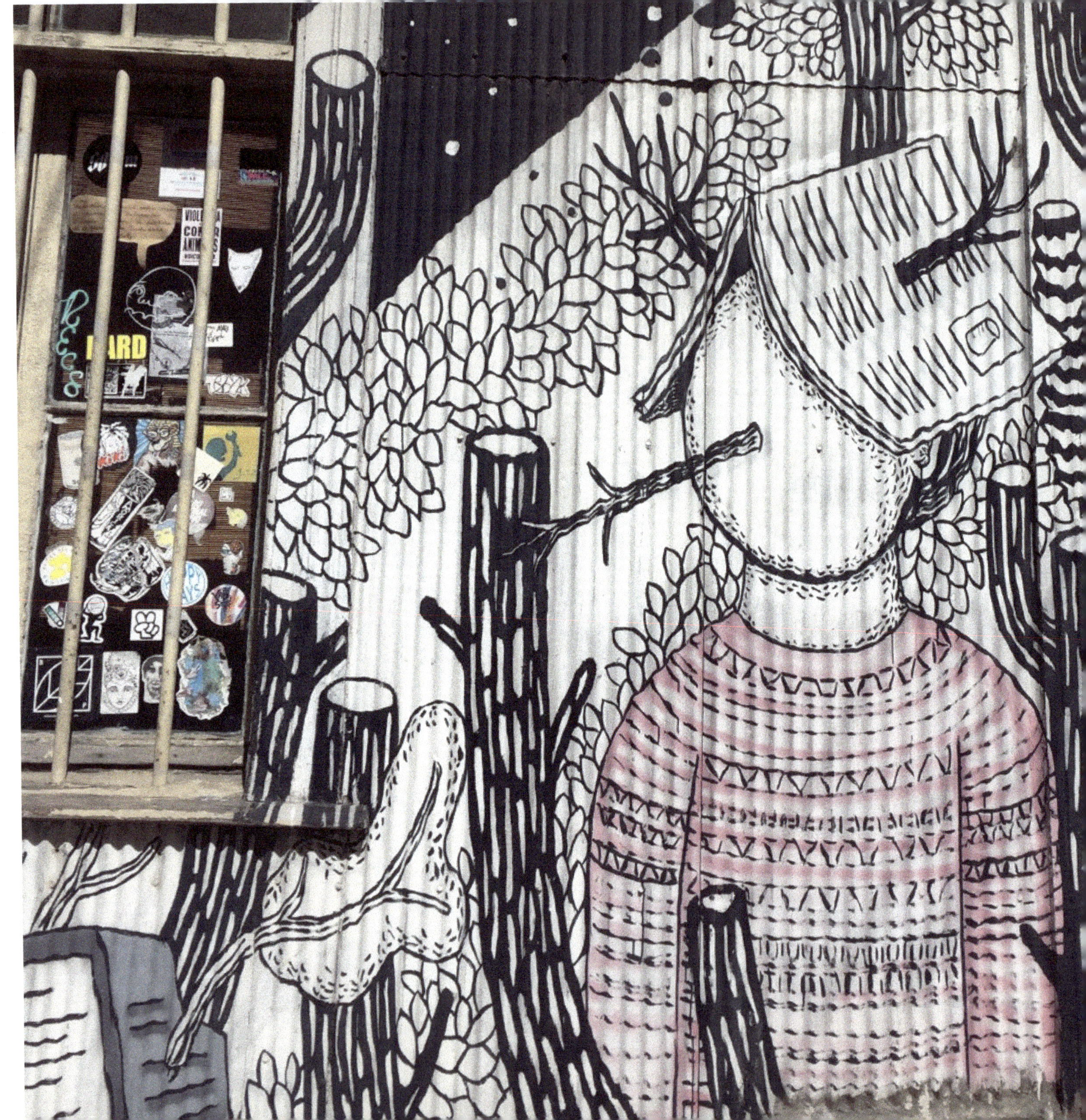

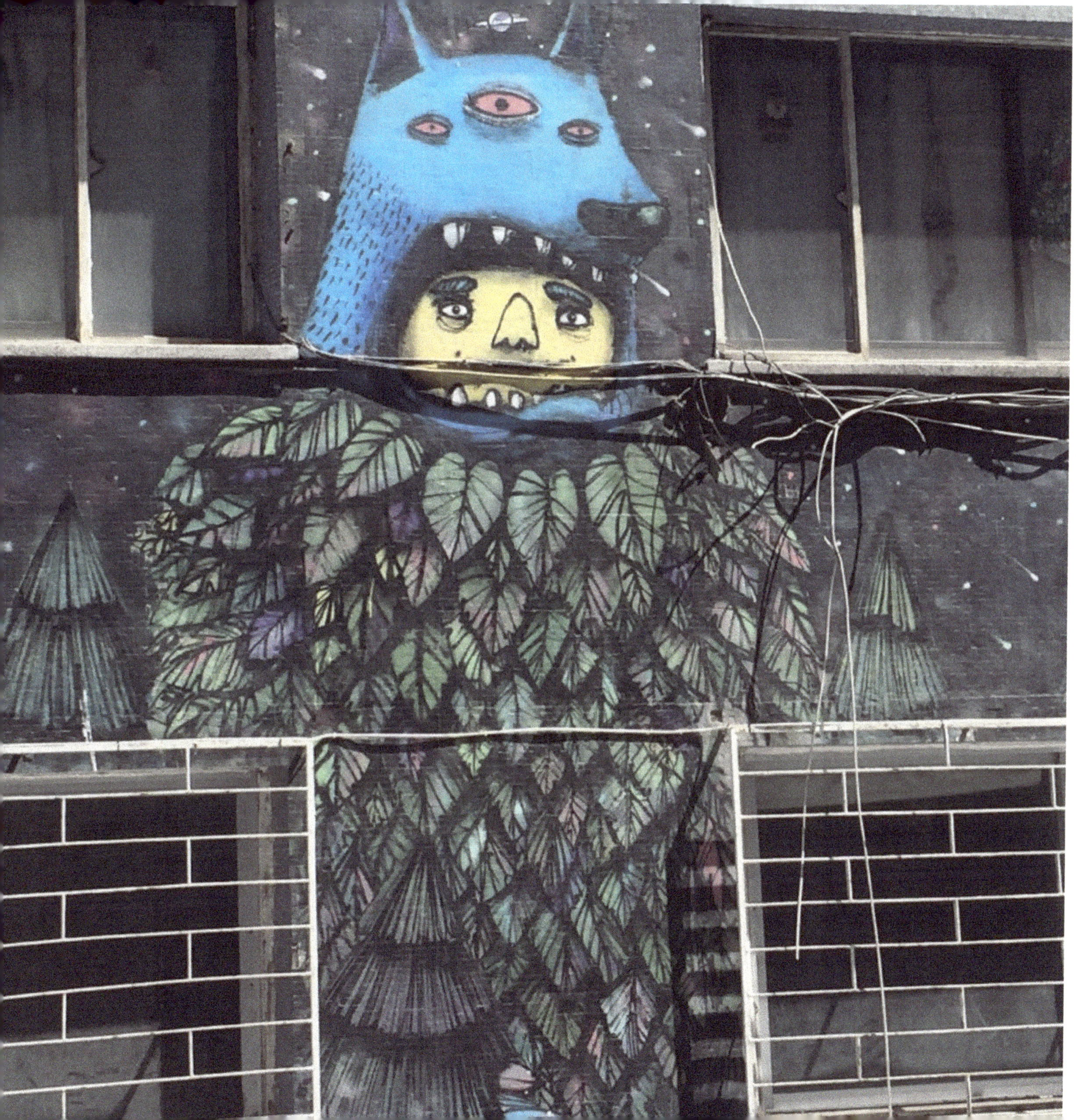

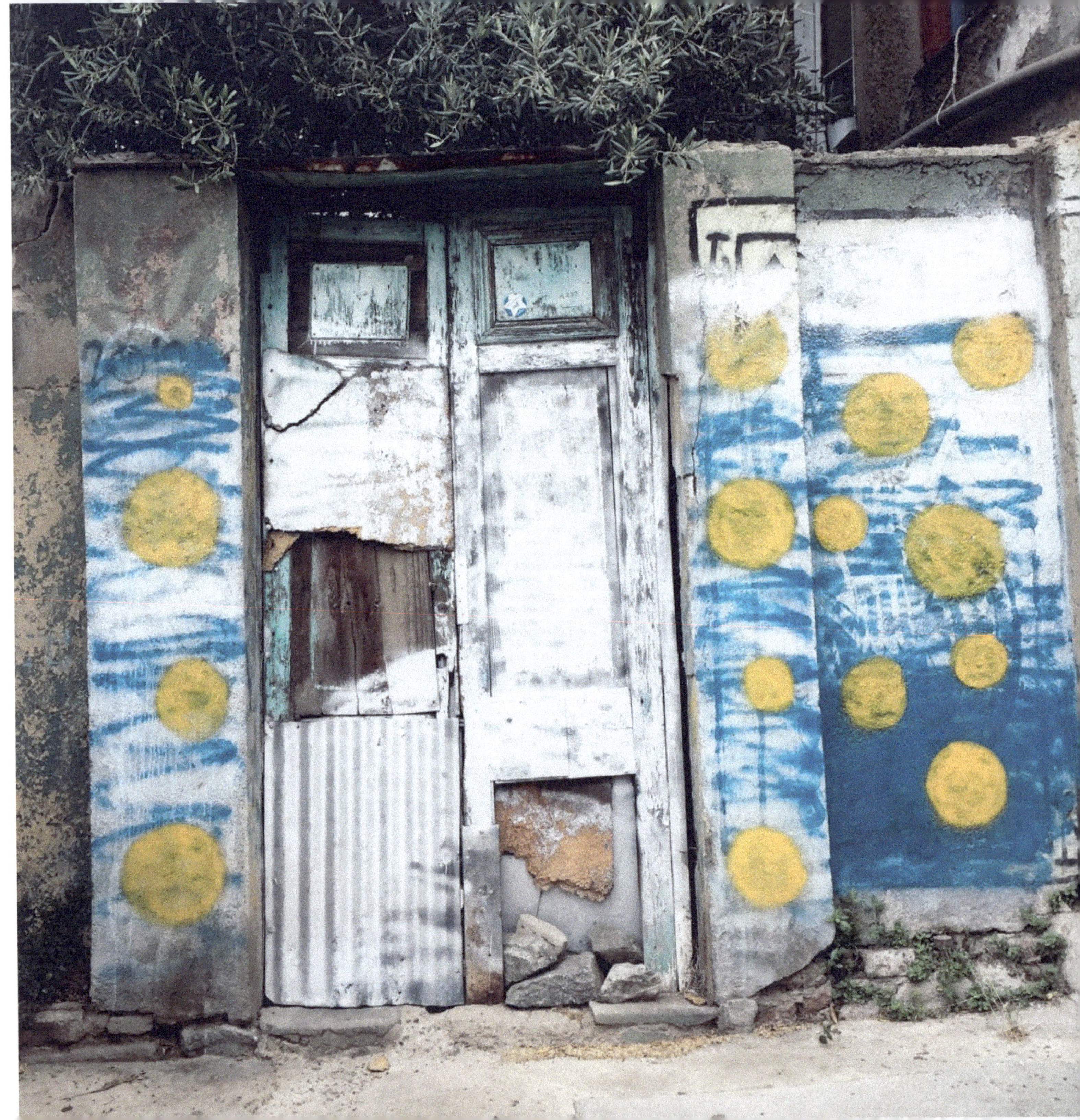

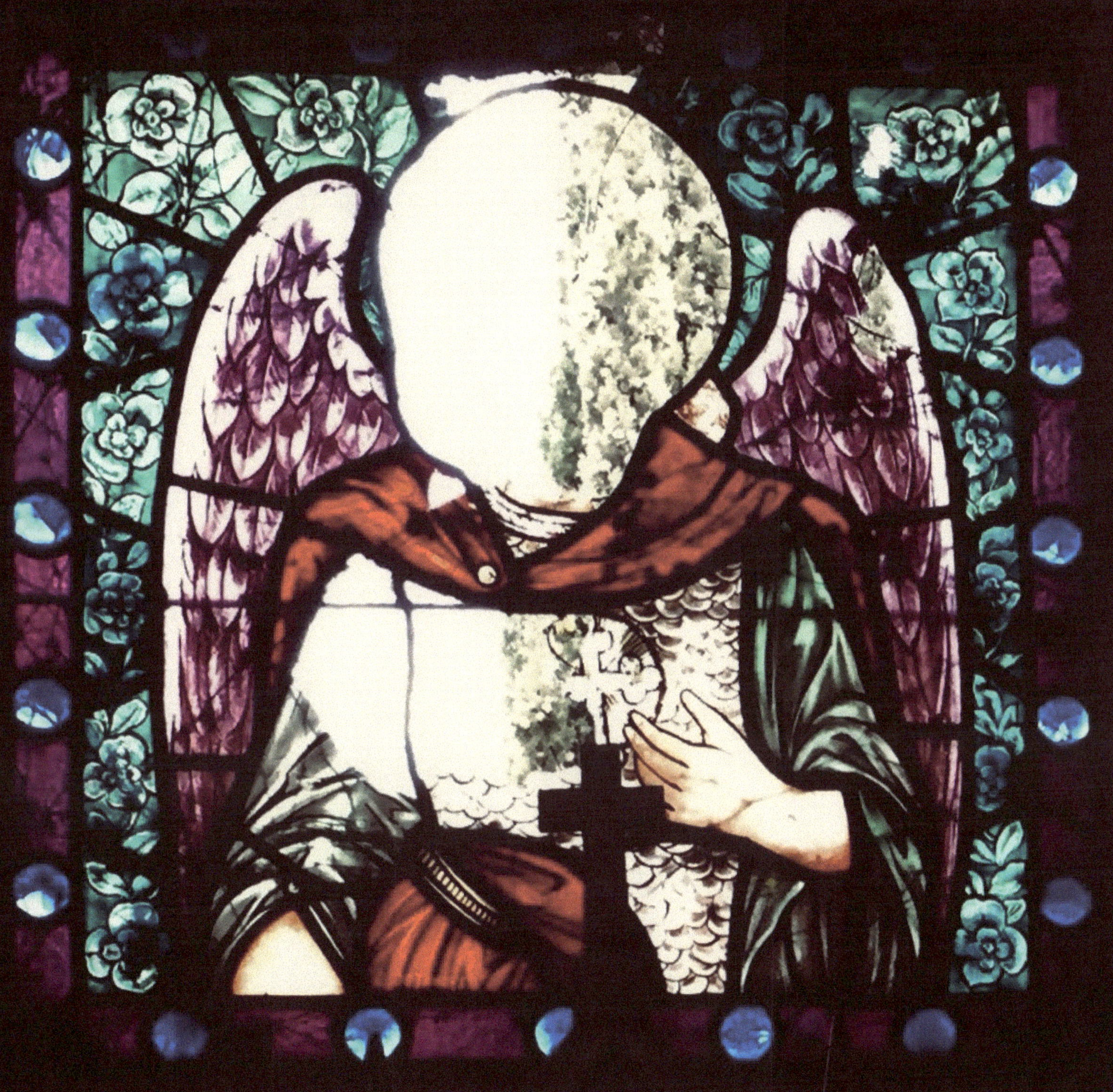

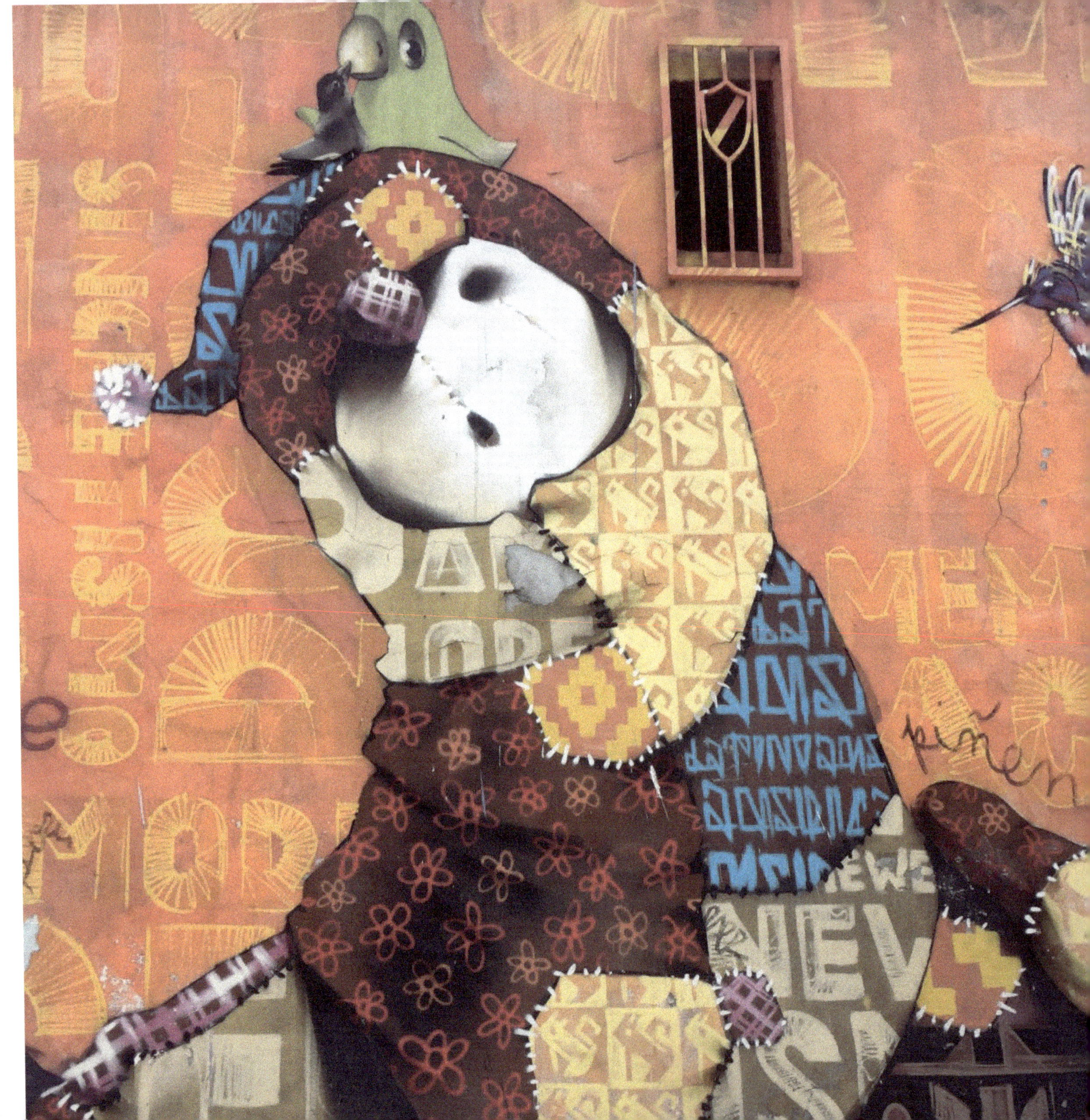

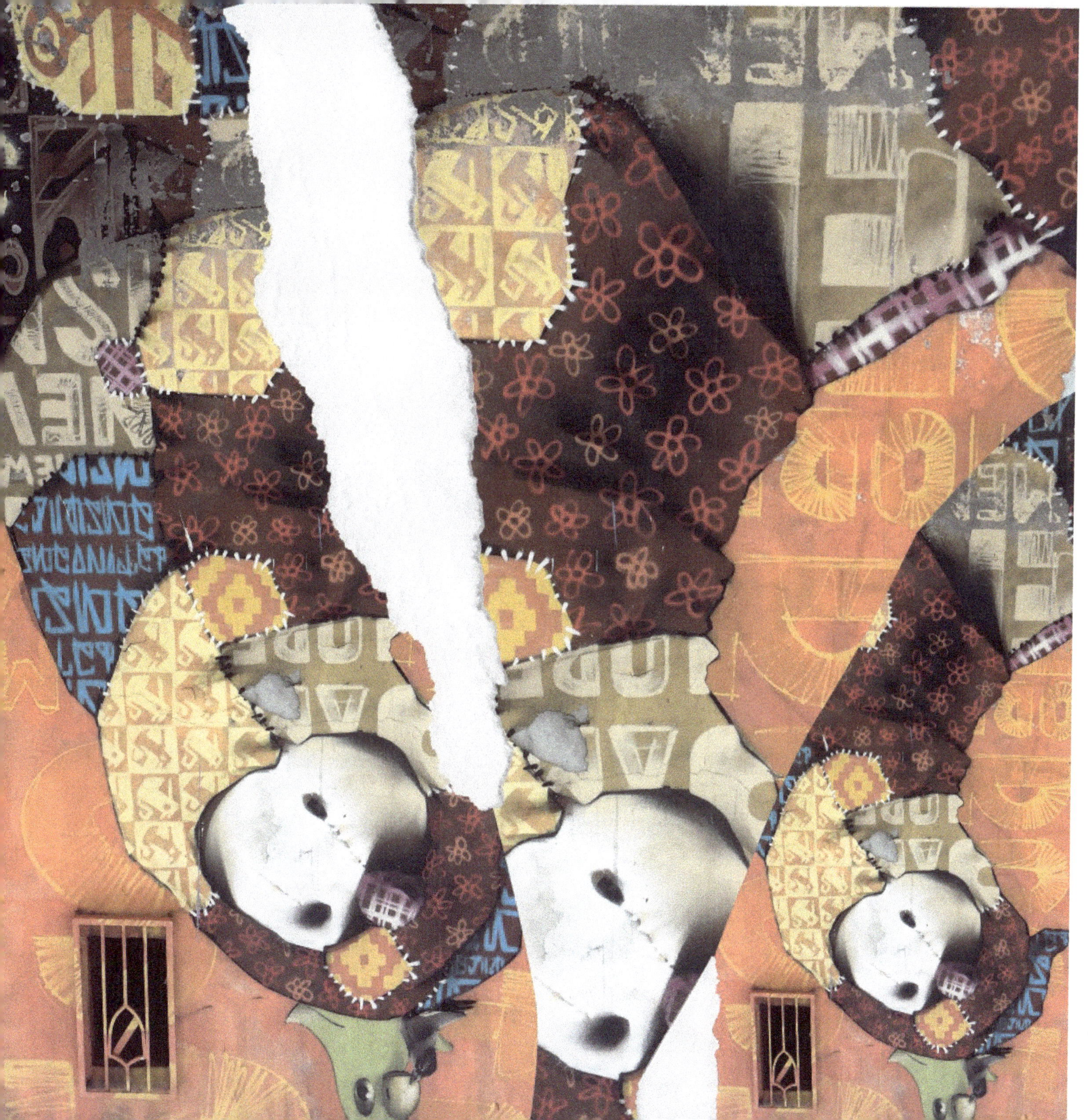